AI Cash Machine

Unlock the Profit Power of AI to Transform Businesses, Launch Profitable Startups, and Create Personal Wealth

Brendan C

Contents

Introduction

What if you could crack the code to the next big thing that's already here? What if you held a golden key that opened the door to unprecedented business growth, entrepreneurial innovation, and personal financial success?

In this introduction, we're going to pull back the curtain on one of the most transformative technologies of our time: Artificial Intelligence. This isn't just another buzzword; it's the foundation for your future success, regardless of your background or profession. Prepare to understand why AI is a game-changer, how it's democratizing opportunities, and what actionable insights this book will provide.

Imagine this: you're a painter, but your canvas is a sprawling digital world and your paintbrush is programmed to craft strokes so intricate that they mimic the essence of the human spirit. This is not some pie-in-the-sky vision of the future; it's the reality artists are living today, thanks to AI. We're not talking about replacing human creativity; we're talking about amplifying it. Forget what you've heard about AI being a tool only for scientists or tech giants. It's a tool for you, too.

If you think AI is just about robots and self-driving cars, it's time to reset your compass. AI is in your smartphone, recommending which song you might want to listen to next. It's in healthcare, predicting patient outcomes and aiding in diagnostics. It's even in agriculture, optimizing yields and reducing waste. It's not an understatement to say that AI has infiltrated almost every industry, big or small.

The beauty of AI is not just its scope but its accessibility. Think of AI like the electricity of the 21st century. When electricity became mainstream, it didn't discriminate. Whether you were a baker in a small town or an industrialist in a city, you had access to the same electric power. Similarly, AI is democratizing opportunities, allowing anyone with a computer and internet access to tap into its potential.

Perhaps you're wondering: "Okay, AI is important. But there are a million books out there about it. Why should I stick with this one?" Let's cut through the noise. This book is your treasure map, replete with Xs marking the spot. But instead of cryptic clues, you get actionable insights. Instead of pirate lore, you'll read success stories that prove you don't need to plunder and pillage to find your gold; you just need to know where to dig.

From business growth hacking to launching a startup built around AI technologies—this book is a guide for entrepreneurs eager to disrupt traditional industries. But what about those who haven't yet dipped their toes in the entrepreneurial waters? What if you're still in college, a stay-at-home parent, or someone with a 9-5 job that barely scratches the itch of your latent talents? Don't fret. This book has something for you, too. Not only does it explore businesses built around AI, but it also delves into individual opportunities, side hustles, and even AI-powered personal development.

You might have glanced at the book title, "AI Cash Machine," and wondered if we're over-promising. Far from it! This book isn't about quick get-rich schemes or dubious shortcuts. The "cash machine" metaphor signifies how AI can become a consistent, reliable asset for generating value, much like a well-oiled machine.

How? Well, you don't have to look far for answers. Take the story of Sarah, who used AI algorithms to optimize her online retail store, catapulting her revenues by 50% within three months. Or consider David, who combined his love for storytelling with AI-powered language models to publish bestselling e-books on platforms like Amazon, all while keeping his day job. These people are not computer wizards; they're regular individuals who leveraged AI to create significant financial impact. They turned AI into their own personal cash machines.

This book is about empowering you with that same knowledge. The 'cash' part is only a piece of the equation. The real jackpot is the power of scalability and automation that AI brings, along with the independence and financial security that come as part of the package.

By the end of this introductory journey, you will realize that

AI is more than just a collection of algorithms or an abstract concept reserved for Silicon Valley elites. It's a transformative force that has the potential to level the playing field, whether you are an aspiring entrepreneur, an established business owner, or just a curious soul yearning to accomplish more.

If you want to turn your business into a growth juggernaut or simply amplify your existing talents, AI is your ticket. And this book, dear reader, is your travel guide. Get ready to journey through the realms of possibility, from understanding what AI really is to harnessing its enormous potential for tangible, life-changing results.

As we roll up our sleeves to dig deeper, the first stop on our adventure is unraveling the mystery surrounding AI. What is it, and why should you care? Prepare to be enlightened as we embark on a fascinating exploration that deciphers AI's complexities into bite-sized, understandable pieces. And trust us, this is one journey where every step you take is a step towards a brighter, more successful future.

5

Part I: The AI Primer

What is AI? Unveiling the Mystery

Imagine you're sitting at a café, sipping on your favorite coffee, when suddenly the barista—a human-like robot—starts recommending stocks for you to invest in, accurately predicting the weather for the next month, and composing a poem for you, all in the span of minutes. Sounds like science fiction, right? Yet, this is exactly where artificial intelligence—or AI—could be taking us. And the future might be closer than you think.

In this chapter, we will unravel the elusive concept of artificial intelligence. We'll start with the basic definitions and then delve into the types of AI, highlighting the difference between machine learning and deep learning. Finally, we'll explore why understanding AI is crucial for everyone, not just tech gurus or business tycoons.

1. Basic Definitions: What Exactly is Artificial Intelligence?

So, let's dive in. What is this behemoth called artificial intelligence that we're talking about? Is it just a buzzword, or is it something tangible, something that's already interwoven into our daily lives?

The term "artificial intelligence" often evokes images of

humanoid robots or self-driving cars, but it's so much more than that. Picture this: You're using Google Maps to find the quickest route to a job interview. You punch in the address and, voila, you get real-time traffic updates and ETA. Behind the scenes, algorithms are working at the speed of light to make this happen. That, my friends, is AI at work.

Artificial Intelligence, at its core, is a field in computer science dedicated to creating systems capable of performing tasks that would normally require human intelligence. These tasks range from speech recognition and decision-making to visual perception and language translation. It's like teaching a machine to think, but not just to think—to think smartly.

Why does this matter? Consider your smartphone as an example. How do you think it recognizes your face even when you've just woken up, disheveled and groggy? AI. How does your email service filter spam messages so efficiently? AI again. Your life is already being simplified and optimized by artificial intelligence in ways you might not even realize.

I'd like you to consider AI as a friendly neighborhood Spider-Man. You know he's there, you've seen what he can do, but do you know how he does it? Similarly, AI is around us, making life easier, but understanding how it does this can open doors to unimaginable opportunities. That's what we're going to focus on as we move forward.

Now let's dive into the different types of AI that exist. Trust me, it's not just a monolith; it's a fascinating mosaic of possibilities.

2. Types of AI: Narrow AI vs. General AI vs. Artificial Superintelligence

So, you've heard about AI, but did you know it comes in different flavors? Think of it like ice cream. You've got your classic vanilla, your rich chocolate, and your exotic flavors like matcha or saffron. Similarly, AI can be classified into three broad categories: Narrow AI, General AI, and Artificial Superintelligence.

Let's start with Narrow AI. This is your vanilla flavor, the most common type you'll encounter. Narrow AI is designed to perform a narrow task, like facial recognition or internet searches. Have you ever played a video game against a computer? The computer's ability to play against you is an example of Narrow AI. It's smart, but only in that particular domain.

Now, General AI, or AGI, is where things get interesting. This is your chocolate flavor with extra toppings. AGI has the ability to understand, learn, and apply knowledge across different domains. It can reason, solve problems, and even have emotional understanding. Imagine a robot that can cook, clean, hold a conversation, and beat you in chess, all while composing a symphony! That's AGI for you. Though it's largely theoretical at the moment, its possibility is one of the most exciting (and terrifying) prospects in the field of AI.

Last but not least, there's Artificial Superintelligence. This is your exotic flavor, like dragon fruit mixed with a dash of liquid nitrogen. This form of AI would not just mimic human intelligence; it would surpass it in almost every way—

creativity, problem-solving, emotional intelligence, you name it.

As we navigate through this chapter, think of these categories not just as separate types, but as stages in the evolutionary scale of AI. We're currently at the Narrow AI stage, but we're teetering on the edge of General AI. And who knows? The leap to Artificial Superintelligence could be just around the corner. The question is: are we ready for it? Would you want to live in a world where your coffee-making, poem-composing barista is smarter than you?

But hey, we're getting ahead of ourselves. Before we venture into the philosophical and ethical conundrums, let's keep our feet on the ground and explore what gives AI its "intelligence."

3. Machine Learning: The Brains Behind AI

Remember the old saying, "Rome wasn't built in a day?" Well, AI wasn't built in a day either. It's not just a program that someone writes and then—bam—it's intelligent. The real magic, the secret sauce, if you will, lies in Machine Learning.

If AI were a car, machine learning would be its engine. It's a subfield of AI that provides the system with the ability to learn from experience. Imagine you're teaching a child to recognize different shapes. The more shapes you show, the better the child gets at identifying them. That's essentially what machine learning algorithms do; they learn from data, identify patterns, and make decisions.

Take Netflix, for example. Ever wondered how it so accurately recommends shows and movies that you're likely to enjoy? It's not just chance; it's machine learning. The algorithm learns from your previous choices, your viewing habits, even the time you spend hovering over a title. It then cross-references this data with that of millions of other users to give you a personalized watchlist.

And it doesn't stop there. Machine learning is the driving force behind many sectors, from healthcare and finance to transportation and e-commerce. When you hear stories about AI detecting cancer earlier than traditional methods or predicting stock market trends, that's machine learning flexing its muscles.

So, why should you care about this? Understanding machine learning is like having a treasure map. Once you know how to read it, the possibilities for discovery are endless. Whether you're a business owner looking to optimize your operations or an individual curious about leveraging AI for personal growth, machine learning is your gateway.

So, here we are, at the end of our introductory journey into the world of AI. We've lifted the veil on what AI is, explored its different types, and peered into the engine that makes it tick: machine learning. But why is any of this important?

Because understanding AI is no longer optional; it's a necessity. It's reshaping industries, revolutionizing how we live, and could potentially redefine what it means to be human. From businesses leveraging AI for unparalleled growth to individuals harnessing its power for personal development—the applications are as varied as they are profound. By the end of this book, you'll not only grasp these concepts but also learn how to apply them, whether you're an entrepreneur, a professional, or just someone fascinated by the limitless potential of AI.

And this, dear reader, is just the tip of the iceberg. There are oceans to sail, and we're just getting started.

Feeling intrigued? Good, because we're about to take this to the next level. While this chapter gave you the "what" of AI, the next chapter, "The Global AI Revolution: Changing the World One Algorithm at a Time," will show you the "why" and the "how." We'll zoom out from the technicalities to give you a panoramic view of how AI is transforming the world. Get ready to have your mind blown. See you in the next chapter!

The Global AI Revolution: Changing the World One Algorithm at a Time

Ever wondered how a single search query on Google gets you the answer in less than a second? Or how your phone's facial recognition system recognizes you, even when you've just gotten a haircut? The answer lies in algorithms, the unsung heroes of our daily lives, rapidly transforming not just tech companies but entire industries and countries. We are in the middle of a revolution, one that will change our world as profoundly as the industrial revolution did. Welcome to the AI Revolution.

In this chapter, we're pulling back the curtain on the scale and scope of AI's influence across various sectors—be it governance, healthcare, finance, or even your daily commute. Through this exploration, you'll begin to grasp just how integral AI is to our modern world and why you should be excited, not afraid, of its transformative power.

How AI is Revolutionizing Healthcare

It's a chilly winter evening, and you're visiting your grandmother who's been struggling with a chronic illness. You're worried as you watch her take an array of pills, hoping that her doctors have finally found the right combination to ease her symptoms. Now, imagine a world where a machine, an AI-powered system, can analyze her medical history, genetics, and even lifestyle factors within seconds to suggest a tailor-made treatment plan with a higher chance of success.

Too good to be true? Not anymore.

The medical field has always been one of ceaseless innovation—from the invention of antibiotics to the advent of MRI scans. But even these remarkable advancements often face limitations, especially when it comes to treating complicated and multi-faceted diseases like cancer, Alzheimer's, or diabetes. This is where AI steps in like a quiet superhero.

You've probably heard about IBM's Watson, which defeated human champions on the game show "Jeopardy!" But did you know Watson has a new job now? It's working with oncologists to identify potential cancer treatments. Watson can scan millions of medical journals, clinical trial data, and patient records within seconds, a task that would take humans years to complete.

But it's not just about quickly processing large amounts of data; it's about the depth of analysis that AI can provide. Imagine AI as an extremely proficient detective, only instead of solving crimes, it's solving medical mysteries. It can find correlations and patterns among diverse datasets, even those that appear unrelated at a cursory glance. This detective works 24/7, tirelessly, giving doctors invaluable insights that can significantly improve patient outcomes.

By leveraging AI's analytical capabilities, healthcare

professionals are gaining a more holistic view of disease mechanisms, leading to the discovery of novel treatment pathways. This is the first step towards personalized medicine, where treatment plans are not one-size-fits-all but uniquely tailored to each individual's genetic makeup and lifestyle.

The applications are boundless. From automated radiology that can detect anomalies in X-rays with unprecedented accuracy to AI-powered wearable devices that monitor heart rates and predict cardiac events, the medical field is undergoing a seismic shift. It's a transformation that's reducing not just the medical errors but also the skyrocketing healthcare costs.

And we're just scratching the surface here. The applications of AI in healthcare are as vast as they are game-changing. For patients, it could mean more accurate diagnoses, less invasive treatments, and even the dream of preventive healthcare becoming a reality.

AI in Governance: Policing, Policy-making, and More

Picture this: you're a city planner, and you've just been handed the reins to design an urban infrastructure that's both efficient and sustainable. You're grappling with a multitude of challenges—traffic congestion, waste management, emergency response systems, and public safety. You've got data, sure, but it's like having thousands of puzzle pieces and not knowing how to fit them together to create a coherent picture.

Enter Artificial Intelligence.

Much like a seasoned chess player thinks several moves ahead, AI algorithms can forecast urban challenges before they escalate into problems. But these aren't your run-of-the-mill forecasts; we're talking about predictive models that account for a dizzying array of variables, from weather patterns to human behavior.

Consider crime prevention. Traditional policing often involves officers patrolling neighborhoods and reacting to criminal activities. With AI, law enforcement can now predict which areas are more likely to witness criminal behavior, allowing for preventative measures to be put in place. Imagine a world where the majority of crimes are stopped before they even happen. It's not a scene from a sci-fi movie; it's a rapidly approaching reality.

But what about the policymakers, the people behind the curtains of governance? They're no strangers to challenges—whether it's deciding on economic reforms, healthcare policies, or educational initiatives. Their decisions impact millions, and a slight misstep can have cascading effects on society. AI offers these decision-makers a robust toolkit for data-driven governance.

For instance, AI can simulate the economic repercussions of a proposed tax change, taking into account not just the macroeconomic indicators but also the nuanced interactions between various sectors. Think of it as an elaborate domino setup, where AI anticipates how one domino's fall will impact the others, helping policymakers understand the full scope of their decisions before they take the plunge.

It's not just about the decisions that are being made but also the transparency behind them. AI algorithms can sift through historical data to identify patterns of success and failure in previous policies. This not only makes the policy-making process more transparent but also sets the stage for accountability, an element often missing in governance.

Yet, it's crucial to tread carefully. Like any tool, AI is only as good as the hands that wield it. The potential for misuse or unintended consequences is real—be it through biased algorithms that perpetuate societal inequities or invasive surveillance systems that impede on individual freedoms.

In essence, the promise of AI in governance is not about replacing human judgment but enhancing it. It's about creating a more just, efficient, and accountable system that serves the public good.

AI: The Maestro Behind Your Playlist and Binge-Watching Nights

Remember the days of burning CDs, creating mixtapes, or waiting for that one song to play on the radio? Or how about flipping through TV channels hoping to stumble upon something interesting? Those days are almost unimaginable now. Thanks to AI, you're just a click away from a playlist that feels like it's curated by your best friend or a recommended TV series that you'll end up binge-watching.

Ah, the nostalgia of the past! Yet, we've entered a digital

renaissance, orchestrated by AI, that has heightened our entertainment experience to levels we couldn't have fathomed just a decade ago. AI algorithms sift through billions of data points, learning your habits, preferences, and even your mood swings, to serve you the content that resonates with you. It's like having a personal DJ and a movie critic residing inside your device, eagerly waiting to match your current vibe with the perfect tune or flick.

Here's the kicker: it's not just the algorithms that work in the background, AI is entering the creative process itself. Films are being edited, music composed, and art created by AI technologies. This doesn't eliminate the human touch but augments it, enabling artists to explore new avenues they never thought possible. AI is not a usurper; it's a collaborator.

In the grand tapestry of entertainment, the threads of AI are interwoven so deeply that pulling it apart would unravel innovations we now take for granted. So the next time you effortlessly find a new favorite song or show, tip your hat to the AI silently working in the background, making your leisure hours infinitely more enjoyable.

Your "aha" moments of discovering a new artist or a gripping series aren't mere luck; they're engineered serendipities, fine-tuned to your liking by intricate algorithms. These algorithms get better with every click, every skipped song, and every "thumbs up." It's a relationship where you and the AI feed off each other's choices, creating a highly personalized universe of entertainment.

And let's not overlook the business side. The entertainment industry, with its fierce competition, has turned to AI for improving not just content delivery but content creation and marketing. Predictive analytics, driven by AI, help producers and marketers understand what kind of content will become the next big hit, be it a summer blockbuster or a sleeper indie success.

So, as you hit 'play' on that eerily accurate playlist or find yourself gripped by a series you never thought you'd like, know that there's a silent maestro at work. The real magic? You don't see it, but you definitely feel it. It's an unseen, often unacknowledged, revolution that makes our 'play' button so much more than just a play button.

By taking a deep dive into AI's impact on entertainment, you're not just flipping the lid on your TV box or music app; you're pulling back the curtain on a technological marvel that learns, evolves, and personalizes, creating a new world of entertainment that is as unique as you are.

AI: The Game Changer in Sports and Physical Entertainment

The marvels of AI aren't just confined to the digital screens of our computers or televisions; they stretch into the very arenas and stadiums that have long been the battlegrounds of human physical prowess. Imagine a world where AI not only helps athletes train but also enhances the spectator experience in unimaginable ways. You don't have to imagine too hard; we are living it.

The next time you marvel at a jaw-dropping move by a basketball player or a tactical masterstroke in a soccer game, remember, AI might have had a hand (or algorithm) in that. AI analyzes player statistics, team formations, and even tracks player movements in real-time to offer insights that were previously either impossible or extremely time-consuming to obtain. We're talking Moneyball on steroids.

But the AI influence doesn't stop at the athlete or the coach; it waltzes through the stands, making its way to you, the spectator. Enhanced real-time analytics give commentators the tools to provide much deeper insights during a game, making your experience as a viewer more enriching. Imagine augmented reality overlays showing a soccer player's real-time heart rate or a basketball player's shooting angle, all in real-time. Yes, it's happening.

This goes beyond the wow factor; it has democratized the field. Smaller teams and individual athletes can now get access to high-level analytics and training regimes that were once the sole domain of wealthy clubs. At the heart of this democratization? Affordable AI solutions that are as ubiquitous as smartphones.

Speaking of smartphones, AI algorithms in your favorite sports apps update you not just on the scores but predict future game outcomes, player performance, and much more. They serve you tailored sports news and even let you be the coach in fantasy sports, giving you an immersive experience that was inconceivable a few years ago.

We are at a junction where technology isn't just an add-on; it's becoming integral to the game—be it in the way athletes train, how games are played, or how we, as fans, engage with our favorite sports. It's as though AI has bought a ticket to the game, and it's sitting right next to you, whispering invaluable insights into your ear.

As you delve further into the influence of AI in various facets of life, from healthcare to governance, and now sports and entertainment, it becomes evident that we are not just witnesses but active participants in a revolution. A revolution that's redefining not just what technology can do, but what it means to be human in an increasingly automated world.

So the next time you cheer for your favorite team, or find yourself engrossed in a game, remember, it's not just the athletes who've upped their game; it's the entire ecosystem, supercharged by the unseen, but omnipresent force of AI.

As we wrap up our journey through the AI-augmented stadiums and sports arenas, your mind might already be racing with ideas about the limitless possibilities of AI in different areas of life. Your excitement is warranted; this technology is not a distant reality but an ever-present companion, shaping our experiences and future. In the upcoming chapter, we'll venture further, exploring how these AI systems are pushing the boundaries of what's possible in ways you may not even have considered yet—especially in business, the driving force of our modern world. Stay with us; you won't want to miss what's coming next.

Zooming Into the Future: The Sky's Not the Limit

Picture this: It's 2040, and you're in a self-driving car that not only knows the fastest route but also your favorite song to listen to when you're stuck in traffic. Just as you settle in, your AI-powered virtual assistant informs you that your biometrics suggest you might be getting sick—perhaps something you ate—and recommends a detour to a healthcare center that can provide a quick diagnosis. This isn't a sci-fi novel; this could be our reality.

The Advent of AI in Daily Life: From Home to Outer Space

We already brushed the surface when we spoke about AI in healthcare, governance, and sports. But those applications are just the tip of the iceberg. Think about your daily life for a moment: the way you wake up, get ready, go to work, engage with friends, and even how you relax—it's all being gradually transformed by AI.

The AI-driven home is no longer just a page from a retro-futuristic comic book; it's quickly becoming the standard. From energy-efficient, AI-controlled homes that know when to turn up the thermostat to cooking appliances that can whip up your favorite meal just by analyzing a picture you took at a restaurant, the possibilities are limitless.

How would you feel about a refrigerator that knows exactly when you're running low on milk and automatically places an order for you? Convenience at its peak, isn't it? And it's not just terrestrial life that AI is transforming. It's paving the way for efficient space exploration as well. Imagine rockets that make real-time, data-driven decisions on the path to take, saving fuel and increasing the chances of a successful mission. The future isn't just near; it's already unfolding before our eyes.

In this ever-transforming landscape, one can't help but wonder what the future holds. And while predictions may vary, one thing is certain: AI is not just a wave—it's a tsunami, ready to transform everything in its path.

Merging Man and Machine: The Ethics and Reality of Cyborg Technologies

Let's consider a hypothetical scenario for a moment. You're at work, and you notice a colleague showing off her new smartwatch, which can not only track her health metrics but also allows her to control her home's lighting, thermostat, and even her car. It's impressive, but it's not that different from what we have today. Now imagine if, instead of a smartwatch, she had a chip implanted in her hand that could do all that and more.

This isn't some futuristic fantasy. Researchers are already exploring brain-computer interfaces, prosthetic limbs controlled by thought, and even AI-driven organ replacements. The line between man and machine is blurring, and while this opens up incredible possibilities, it also brings us to an ethical crossroad. Do we have the right to modify human biology to such an extent? How do we prevent these advancements from becoming exclusive privileges of the wealthy? The ethical questions are as infinite as the potential applications.

Imagine a world where 'upgrading' your body parts becomes as normal as upgrading your smartphone. It might sound like the stuff of science fiction, but the technologies in development today could make it a reality in the coming decades. What does that mean for the idea of 'humanity'? Are we moving towards a new definition of what it means to be human?

The impact extends beyond just our physical selves. What about our minds? AI can already mimic many human cognitive functions. What happens when we have the technology to enhance human intelligence artificially? Would that create an insurmountable divide between those who are enhanced and those who are not?

In this accelerating torrent of technological development, we can't afford to ignore the ethical implications. Who gets to make these decisions? How do we make them inclusive and fair? And most importantly, how do we balance the remarkable benefits against the ethical and societal costs?

As we stand on this threshold, it's crucial to not only embrace the technological possibilities but also understand the responsibilities that come with them. The cyborg future is fascinating but fraught, and how we navigate this ethical maze will shape not just technology but the very essence of human civilization.

The Coming Wave of Machine-Designed Medicines

Pharmaceutical research has long been the purview of highly trained specialists, working in multi-billion-dollar labs, sifting through years of biological data, and conducting endless trials. However, AI is set to turn this paradigm on its head. Already, algorithms can analyze biochemical interactions at speeds unattainable by human researchers, predicting outcomes and suggesting modifications. This is more than just speeding up the research process; it's a fundamental shift in how we approach medicine itself.

Imagine a personalized healthcare system where medicines are designed on a patient-by-patient basis, where an AI analyzes your specific genetic makeup, lifestyle, and even your daily routine to concoct a treatment tailor-made for you. It's not about treating symptoms or even diseases; it's about treating individuals. This vision could upend our entire understanding of 'wellness.'

However, the flip side to this is disconcerting. How would such power be regulated? Could an algorithm mistakenly generate a harmful substance? And again, who gets access to these personalized treatments? If it's costly to generate individualized medicine, we risk creating a healthcare system that's even more unequal than it already is. Will your financial standing decide whether you're eligible for the most effective treatments?

The AIs That 'Know' You

But let's not stop at just physical changes; the frontier of AI also extends into the realm of the mind. AI-driven systems are becoming increasingly adept at analyzing human emotions and thoughts. We've all seen the tip of this iceberg: algorithms that recommend what movie to watch, what food to order, or even who you should date. But what happens when these algorithms get exponentially better, to the point where they know you better than you know yourself?

Here, the ethical quandaries are startling. Imagine a marketing algorithm so good at its job that it can manipulate your purchasing decisions effortlessly. Or a surveillance system so adept at interpreting human emotion that it can predict and report 'problematic' behavior before a crime is committed. It's a scenario that starts to look like Minority Report, except it's not just the government you have to worry about; it's every corporation, marketer, or even a nefarious individual armed with potent AI tools.

In each of these future scenarios—whether it's upgrading your body, personalizing your medicine, or algorithms that 'know' you—the opportunities are thrilling but tinged with ethical complexities. Our ability to harness these technologies will dictate the landscape of the future, affecting how we live, how society operates, and even what it means to be human.

As we close this chapter, we're about to venture into an even more practical realm: how AI is impacting businesses today and what opportunities it presents for entrepreneurs and even individuals looking to leverage this transformative technology. From understanding the global revolution, we're about to zoom into how you can be a part of this seismic shift, in the boardroom or even your living room.

Part II: Business and AI: A Match Made in Silicon]

Unlocking Business Growth with AI: The Secret Sauce

Imagine a world where your business operations are so finely tuned that you can predict customer behaviors, streamline your logistics to the last cent, and market your products in a way that seems almost psychic. What if we told you this world isn't in the realm of science fiction but can be your reality, all thanks to Artificial Intelligence?

AI as the New Competitive Advantage

Let's be clear: the business world is a battlefield. Every player seeks that elusive, game-changing strategy that propels them into new echelons of success. Enter AI, the 21st-century sword, and shield of the corporate gladiator. Why a sword and a shield, you ask? A sword because AI cuts through the dense forest of big data to provide actionable insights. A shield because, in a volatile market, knowledge is your best defense.

But to comprehend the depth of AI's influence, you must first accept that we've moved past the Industrial Age. We are in the Information Age, a period where the one who holds the most accurate information holds power. Think of AI as your advisor, akin to the oracles of ancient civilizations but rooted in hard data and capable of evolving in real-time.

You may not need to know the future, but you do need to understand trends, consumer behaviors, and market flux. AI provides that for you. It's like having a weather vane that not only tells you which way the wind is blowing but can predict hurricanes, tell you the best time to sail, and even suggest how to build a more efficient boat.

The businesses that adopt AI aren't just staying ahead of the curve; they're drawing a new curve altogether. Companies like Amazon aren't giants because they're lucky; they're giants because they've incorporated AI into everything from customer recommendations to supply chain management. The phrase "adapt or die" has never been more relevant.

So how do you go about incorporating AI into your business? Slowly. Think of it as adding spices to a dish. You wouldn't pour an entire jar of paprika into your stew, right? Similarly, the integration of AI should be gradual, tested at each stage, and adjusted according to the feedback and results.

AI isn't a magic wand; it's a tool, perhaps the most potent one in your toolbox. But like any tool, its effectiveness depends on the skill of the person wielding it. It requires an understanding of your business needs, a clear vision of what you want to achieve, and the willingness to adapt and learn.

But be warned, the clock is ticking. Every day you're not utilizing AI, you're falling behind. Your competitors aren't waiting, so neither should you.

Real-World Applications: Case Studies

Let's not wade in the shallows; it's time to plunge into the depths. Imagine you're in a museum, staring at different paintings, each representing a company's journey with AI. As you wander through this gallery of corporate innovation, the images aren't static; they come alive with the brilliance of transformation.

Take Netflix as our first portrait. It's not just a streaming service; it's a data-driven behemoth. How many times have you thought, "Just one more episode," only to find yourself binge-watching an entire season? That's no accident. Netflix uses AI algorithms to understand your viewing habits, recommend shows that you're likely to enjoy, and even decide what content to produce next. It's like a chef who not only knows what you want to eat but also invents new dishes you didn't know you'd love. And what's the result? Viewer engagement skyrockets, and so does subscription revenue.

Or look at Shopify, the canvas painted in hues of entrepreneurial spirit. With the help of AI, Shopify can suggest products to online shoppers with an eerie accuracy, like a seasoned salesperson who knows just what you're looking for. AI in Shopify isn't just an add-on; it's woven into the fabric of the user experience, making it not just user-friendly but user-enticing.

Let's talk about a different form of art: Tesla, an amalgamation of engineering and AI, a Mona Lisa in the automotive landscape. Tesla's self-driving cars collect data every second they are on the road. This information is then analyzed to make real-time driving decisions, promising a future where car accidents are as obsolete as floppy disks.

By now, you must be wondering, "How can my business become a masterpiece?" Well, that's the beauty and the challenge; your canvas is blank, and AI is your palette. You can choose your colors, mix them in unique ways, and create a business landscape that's authentically yours. The key? Don't just slap some paint and expect a masterpiece. Plan, experiment, adjust, and most importantly, never stop learning. Each stroke of your brush, powered by AI, will either bring you closer to a corporate Sistine Chapel or a forgotten sketch. The choice is yours.

So, when you're standing at the intersection of decision-making, remember these real-world applications as your signposts. They don't just suggest the way; they illuminate a path paved with gold—both metaphorically and financially.

Decision-making Refined by Data Analytics

Imagine steering a ship in the middle of the ocean with no compass, maps, or even the stars to guide you. That's what decision-making in business can feel like without the right data. AI isn't just your compass; it's your modern-day GPS, offering the quickest, safest, and most efficient route to your destination—success. Data analytics powered by AI can sift through oceans of data to fetch you pearls of insights that are otherwise hidden.

Consider a company like Netflix. Do you think it's just luck that they seem to know what show will keep you binge-watching all weekend? Not at all. Their recommendation engine uses sophisticated algorithms to analyze your viewing patterns, compare them with similar profiles, and then suggest shows that you're likely to enjoy. They make the decision-making process look so effortless, but behind the scenes, it's a rigorous exercise in data analytics.

Companies like Google have even mastered the art of predictive analytics, which is like a crystal ball but grounded in data. They can predict what you're likely to search for, click on, or even buy online, offering invaluable insights to marketers.

In essence, when you integrate AI and data analytics into your decision-making processes, you're not just shooting arrows in the dark and hoping one hits the mark. You're more like an Olympic archer, who knows the direction and strength of the wind, the curve of the bow, the weight of the arrow, and the distance to the target, aiming with precision that comes from insight and practice.

Customer Engagement through Personalization

Remember walking into a store and the salesperson not only remembers your name but also what you bought last time and what you might be interested in today? That's the level of personalization customers now expect online, and AI delivers just that, but at a scale unimaginable in a brick-and-mortar store.

With AI algorithms, Amazon isn't just a marketplace; it's a

personalized shopping assistant. "You might also like," isn't just a suggestion; it's an educated guess about what could make your life better or more enjoyable. From AI chatbots that address your queries in real-time to personalized email marketing campaigns that don't just end up in spam folders, AI can engage customers in ways that were previously only possible in one-on-one interactions.

Optimizing Logistics and Operations

If decision-making is the brain of a business, logistics and operations are its beating heart. It's all about getting the right things to the right places at the right time, and there's zero room for error. But let's face it, humans are prone to error. That's where AI steps in.

Imagine a symphony where every musician knows precisely when to play their note. AI ensures your logistics and operations are just like that—flawless. Companies like UPS have used AI to optimize delivery routes, saving millions of miles of driving every year. The effect? Reduced costs and carbon footprint.

Amazon again serves as an excellent example. Their warehouses are the future—automated with robots, planned down to the last inch, and orchestrated by AI algorithms that calculate the most efficient use of space and resources.

When you apply AI to logistics and operations, you're not just improving efficiency; you're transforming your business into a well-oiled machine that knows how to adapt, scale, and sustain itself in an ever-changing landscape.

Ethical Considerations in AI Business Applications

You might have noticed that our museum tour of AI in business showcases a utopian vision. It's like a beautifully orchestrated symphony where every note hits perfectly. But what happens when a wrong note is played? What happens when AI, despite its advantages, starts raising ethical eyebrows?

Let's consider facial recognition technology. It sounds promising—a modern version of a security guard who not only knows who should and shouldn't be in the building but also never sleeps, never takes a break. Companies like Clearview AI have been scraping billions of images from the internet to create a tool that can identify a face in a crowd in seconds. It sounds like a science fiction dream, but for many, it's becoming more of a dystopian reality. Privacy advocates are screaming from the rooftops, "What about consent?" If a picture of you is on the internet, does that mean companies have the free reign to use it for their facial recognition databases?

The ethical concerns extend far beyond individual companies. When you have giants like Amazon using AI to predict what you want to purchase next, a question arises— where does predictive modeling end, and manipulation begin? If a machine knows your vulnerabilities, should it exploit them for profit?

These aren't just philosophical debates for armchair ethicists. They're practical, immediate concerns for anyone involved in the world of AI and business. As businesses, your role is akin to that of a conductor. You have to ensure every section of your AI orchestra plays in harmony without hitting a jarring note that disrupts the melody. Ensuring ethical usage of AI isn't a one-time event; it's a continual process, like tuning a piano before every concert.

So, how can you navigate this ethically complex terrain? It starts with asking the right questions and being transparent about your data usage. If you're using customer data to refine your AI algorithms, disclose it. If you're using AI to screen job candidates, make sure the software isn't inadvertently biased against certain demographic groups. It's a wild, wild west out there in the realm of AI ethics, and the sheriff that's going to enforce the law has to be you.

You see, ethics in AI isn't an abstract painting that's open to interpretation; it's more like a detailed blueprint—each line meticulously drawn, each angle carefully calculated. Ignore this blueprint, and your AI project can quickly turn into a leaning tower that not only tilts but also risks collapsing altogether.

We've traversed through the beautiful landscapes and stumbled upon the cautionary tales of our AI museum. It's a rich tapestry, and as with any great art, it's continuously evolving. One thing is certain, though—whether you're an entrepreneur, a tech geek, or someone fascinated by the ever-changing dynamics between AI and business, it's a museum worth revisiting time and again.

Having explored the transformative power of AI in decision-making, customer engagement, and operations, you may be wondering how all these elements coalesce into a business model. It's one thing to adopt AI tools, but how do you structure an entire business around them? Our next chapter will pull back the curtain on the frameworks that trailblazing companies have implemented. Prepare to delve into the architectures that make it financially viable to build a business in the age of AI.

AI-Driven Business Models: The Blueprint for Financial Success

Have you ever wondered why companies like Netflix, Tesla, and Amazon seem to be living in the future while everyone else is catching up? They're not just companies; they're AI-driven powerhouses. But how did they get there? In this chapter, we're diving deep into the heart of AI-driven businesses—their business models. From subscriptions to freemium strategies, we'll unpack how you can turn AI capabilities into fiscal achievements.

The Evolution of Business Models in the AI Era

In the not-so-distant past, businesses ran on grit, instinct, and the famous 4Ps (Price, Product, Place, Promotion). Fast-forward to today, and the landscape is almost unrecognizable. We've added some new tenants to the business cathedral—data, algorithms, and automated decision-making.

Think about Netflix. At its inception, Netflix was a DVD rental service, practically a Blockbuster-by-mail. But by leveraging big data and AI, they transitioned into a subscription-based streaming behemoth. Their AI algorithms don't just recommend what you should watch; they even influence what gets produced. "House of Cards," anyone?

The lesson? AI isn't an accessory to your business model; it can be the business model.

Imagine, then, if your business could anticipate customer needs before they even articulate them. Or adjust prices based on supply and demand in real-time. This isn't science fiction; this is today, and businesses who adopt AI-driven models are the ones writing the future.

Why Subscription Models Are the New Black

Stepping into the realm of subscription models feels like entering a bustling, futuristic marketplace, except this marketplace is online, and it's open 24/7. The subscription economy isn't new; magazines and newspapers have been using it for decades. But what is new is the injection of AI, transforming these subscriptions into something far more dynamic and personalized.

Take the New York Times for instance. A venerable institution in journalism, it initially resisted the digital wave, clinging to print. Then came the pivot to digital, followed by a subscription model. Now, it's not just about publishing articles online. Their AI algorithms analyze your reading habits, time spent on each article, and even how far you scroll down. This isn't merely to serve you better recommendations but to dynamically adapt its paywall, making you an offer that's hard to refuse when you've hit your monthly free article limit.

But perhaps no company exemplifies the magic of subscription models paired with AI better than Amazon Prime. Ever wonder why Amazon recommends just the thing you didn't know you needed? That's their AI at work. These models know more than just what you've bought; they know what you almost bought, what you lingered on, what you put in your cart and then abandoned. Combine that intelligence with a subscription model, and you've got a powerhouse that keeps customers coming back.

The genius of AI-driven subscription models lies in their mutability. Prices aren't just set; they're adapted in real time. Packages aren't just created; they evolve as customer preferences do. With AI, your subscription offering isn't static; it's a living, breathing entity that learns from every interaction, constantly improving, refining, and yes—upselling.

AI is like the orchestra conductor, ensuring that all elements of your subscription service are harmoniously tuned to the individual user, down to the last detail. That's how you captivate your audience; not by making everyone listen to the same symphony, but by giving each listener their unique melody.

The Freemium Dance: The Tango of Temptation and Conversion

Ah, the freemium model—where customers are lured in by the allure of "free" and kept hooked by the promise of "premium." It's like a well-choreographed dance, a tango between temptation and conversion. And in this dance, AI is your star choreographer.

Imagine walking into a café where the aroma of freshly brewed coffee is in the air. You're offered a free cup, and just as you're relishing that first sip, the barista (let's call him "AI") suggests, "Would you like some freshly baked pastries to go with your coffee?" But here's the catch: the pastries aren't free. Welcome to the Freemium Café.

Companies like Spotify and Dropbox have executed this dance with finesse. Spotify lets you listen to music for free but intersperses your playlists with ads. The moment you show signs of annoyance—perhaps skipping ads too fast or muting them—AI steps in. "For just $9.99 a month, you can listen ad-free," it whispers, and many of us take the bait.

In the world of software, companies like Dropbox offer basic storage space for free but reserve advanced features for paying customers. Their AI monitors how close you are to reaching your free storage limit, and as you teeter on the edge, it swoops in with promotional pricing for extra space—just when you need it.

The beauty of the freemium model driven by AI lies in its ability to "read the room," to understand when a user is most susceptible to parting with their money for added convenience or capabilities. It's like a dance instructor who knows when you're ready for the next intricate step, guiding you seamlessly from a basic waltz to a riveting tango.

And then there are the gaming industries like Fortnite, where the game itself is free, but the outfits, the skins, the dances? Ah, those will cost you. AI carefully observes your playing style, the characters you choose, the virtual rooms you enter, and subtly suggests items that could enhance your experience. Before you know it, you're not just playing a free game; you're emotionally and financially invested.

If run-of-the-mill subscription models are akin to arranged marriages—stable but often lacking in spontaneity—freemium models are the whirlwind romances, fueled by passion and the thrill of the new. They offer a taste of the high life, enough to whet your appetite but not to satiate it. And it's AI that plays matchmaker, reading signals that even you weren't aware you were giving off.

So, who leads in this dance? It may appear that the customer does, but in a well-orchestrated freemium model, it's AI that leads, twirls, and dips, always one step ahead, making every move seem like your idea, even when it's not.

Case Study: How Spotify Navigated the Freemium Jungle

Imagine a platform that needs to keep both artists and listeners happy. On one hand, it needs to make revenue, and on the other, it has to keep its vast user base engaged without alienating them with a price point. Spotify's masterstroke was its freemium model, a perfect blend of free access with premium features for those willing to pay.

But here's the twist. Spotify utilized AI to power this freemium model. Through complex machine learning algorithms, Spotify analyses user listening habits, curates playlists, and offers personalized suggestions. This not only keeps the user hooked but also tempts them to explore the ad-free, high-quality streaming available in the premium version. For advertisers, Spotify offers targeted ads based on user preferences, making their freemium model lucrative. This dual-sided strategy, backed by AI-driven insights, ensured Spotify remained profitable while providing massive value to its users.

Dynamic Pricing: The AI Price Tag

Enter a world where the price tag isn't static but fluctuates based on real-time demand, customer preferences, and even external factors like weather or holidays. Welcome to the era of dynamic pricing, made possible by AI.

A classic case is Uber. The price for your ride isn't static but varies depending on demand, traffic conditions, and even events in the vicinity. By processing vast amounts of data in real-time, Uber's algorithms adjust prices to ensure a balance between demand and supply.

Retailers, especially e-commerce giants like Amazon, employ similar strategies. Ever noticed a slight price fluctuation in that gadget you've been eyeing? That's dynamic pricing at work, adjusting prices based on inventory, competitor pricing, and your browsing habits.

AI in B2B: How Companies like Palantir Are Redefining Consultancy

The world of B2B is typically considered rigid, but AI is shaking things up, particularly in the realm of consultancy. Palantir, a public American software company, is at the forefront.

Instead of traditional consultancies, which often rely on historical data and human expertise, Palantir offers platforms that leverage big data for real-time insights. Its software, Gotham, for example, is employed by defense and intelligence agencies to analyze vast troves of data for patterns that a human might overlook.

Similarly, its Foundry platform has found adoption in sectors ranging from pharmaceuticals to aviation, offering companies a bird's-eye view of their operations and suggesting optimizations. By acting as a bridge between raw data and actionable insights, Palantir showcases the immense potential of AI in the B2B landscape.

The Ethical Considerations of AI Business Models

Every silver lining has a cloud, and in the world of AI-driven business models, it's the looming concern of ethics. The capability of AI to collect, analyze, and act on data is unprecedented, but with great power comes great responsibility.

Consider the recommendation algorithms used by platforms like YouTube. While their primary goal is to keep users engaged, they've often been criticized for pushing users down radical or extremist content paths purely based on watch history. Then there's the issue of bias in AI, where algorithms trained on skewed data end up perpetuating stereotypes.

Moreover, the immense data collection capabilities of AI platforms raise privacy concerns. Without clear regulations and ethical boundaries, there's potential for misuse, whether it's in targeted advertising or predictive policing. Brands and platforms need to navigate this minefield carefully, ensuring transparency, user consent, and above all, a commitment to ethical considerations, even if it sometimes means prioritizing them over profitability.

If the previous chapters have taught us anything, it's that AI isn't just a spectator in the corporate arena; it's an MVP playing in multiple positions. Just as it revolutionizes business models, it's also turning traditional marketing and sales strategies on their head. Brace yourself as we delve into the next captivating chapter: "Conquer Marketing and Sales with AI: The Ultimate Strategy." We'll unravel how AI can be your secret weapon to catapult your marketing ROI into the stratosphere, define your customer segments with surgical precision, and sustain customer loyalty in a market where choices abound. Trust me, you'll want to stick around for this.

Conquer Marketing and Sales with AI: The Ultimate Strategy

Picture this: your business is a treasure ship sailing through the stormy seas of the market. You have valuable cargo—your products or services. The maps are your marketing and sales strategies, and your crew consists of your dedicated team. Now, what if I told you that AI is the ultimate compass, ensuring you not only survive the storms but also discover new, uncharted lands filled with opportunities and treasure? That's right. AI can be your North Star in the convoluted world of marketing and sales. Intrigued? Keep reading.

Understanding the AI Marketing Ecosystem

Let's set the stage. Just as an orchestra comprises different instruments, each with a unique role, the AI marketing ecosystem is a symphony of various technologies. From data analytics engines and machine learning algorithms to natural language processing tools, each part contributes to a holistic strategy.

Machine Learning Algorithms: The Maestros

Imagine machine learning algorithms as the conductors of this orchestra, directing the big picture. They analyze vast datasets to recognize patterns and make predictions, guiding your marketing initiatives in the right direction. These aren't just dry, numerical patterns; we're talking about consumer behaviors, seasonal buying trends, and even emotional triggers.

Take Netflix as a case study. Ever wondered why Netflix's recommendations seem to read your mind? The company uses complex machine learning algorithms to analyze your watching history, compare it with millions of other users, and then suggest shows you're likely to enjoy. It's like having a friend who knows your taste but on an industrial scale.

Data Analytics: The Sheet Music

Think of data analytics as the sheet music guiding each instrument in the orchestra. It's the foundational layer that provides raw data for the algorithms to interpret. In marketing, this could mean anything from customer engagement metrics to sales conversion rates. Companies like Adobe are offering sophisticated analytics platforms that integrate seamlessly with AI tools to provide real-time data analysis. This capability allows businesses to adjust their marketing strategies on the fly, ensuring optimal ROI.

Natural Language Processing: The Vocalists

Natural language processing (NLP) plays the vocalist in our AI orchestra, turning data into a language that we can understand. NLP tools analyze customer reviews, social media conversations, and customer service interactions to provide valuable qualitative insights. Have you ever used sentiment analysis to gauge consumer reactions? That's NLP in action.

The Ensemble: Integrated AI Tools

The magic happens when all these components come together to play a harmonious tune, making your marketing more dynamic, more responsive, and more effective. HubSpot, for instance, offers an all-in-one inbound marketing, sales, CRM, and customer service platform, powered by AI functionalities that cover everything we've discussed so far.

To summarize this section, understanding the components of the AI marketing ecosystem is not just beneficial; it's crucial. Just as you wouldn't attend a concert without knowing the orchestra's layout, diving into AI marketing without understanding its elements would be a recipe for discord.

AI in Customer Segmentation

The secret sauce to any successful marketing campaign is knowing your audience. Imagine having a crystal ball that could predict what a customer wants before they even know it themselves. Well, it turns out, you don't need a crystal ball—you need AI.

Consumer Behavior Analysis: The Roots of Segmentation

Customer segmentation is an age-old practice in marketing, but AI breathes new life into it. By leveraging machine learning algorithms, businesses can sift through thousands of data points to identify consumer behaviors at a granular level. But don't mistake this for the 'spray and pray' campaigns of yesteryear. With AI, it's more akin to a skilled archer who can hit the bull's eye every single time.

Take Spotify for example. Ever gotten a playlist recommendation that felt like it was curated just for you? That's AI-driven customer segmentation at work. By analyzing your listening history, skip rates, and even the time of day you listen, Spotify can categorize you into one of several 'audience segments'. Then, it recommends music that suits not just your music taste but also your lifestyle.

Geographic and Demographic Factors

But wait, there's more. AI doesn't just understand behavior; it also considers geographic and demographic data. A winter clothing line can focus on regions experiencing cold weather instead of sending promotions to tropical zones. The targeted approach maximizes the impact while minimizing resources spent.

Let's take a moment to acknowledge the finesse of Amazon here. Have you ever noticed that Amazon seems to know your local holidays, events, or seasons? Its AI systems are trained to identify geographic and demographic nuances to provide an unparalleled personalized shopping experience.

Psychographic Analysis: Deciphering Minds

To get even deeper, AI ventures into psychographic analysis. It taps into attitudes, values, and other psychological metrics to forge a connection with consumers. Luxury brands like Gucci or Porsche don't just target people with high income; they target a mindset—a lifestyle. And AI helps them find this needle in a haystack.

Real-time Segmentation: The Pinnacle of Personalization

AI offers something even more groundbreaking—real-time customer segmentation. Imagine being able to change your marketing strategy instantly based on real-time customer interactions. As soon as someone engages with your website or social media, AI algorithms kick in to analyze this fresh data, allowing you to tailor your marketing strategies instantaneously.

In essence, AI-powered customer segmentation is like having a fleet of top-tier marketing consultants who are perpetually tuned into the desires and behaviors of your target audience, operating in real-time, all the time.

By now, you should be envisioning the transformative potential AI can bring to your customer segmentation strategies. But let's not just stop here; let's turn our attention to how AI can supercharge your ROI in marketing. Ready?

Supercharging ROI with AI

ROI—three simple letters that carry the weight of the world for marketers and business leaders. The eternal quest for maximizing returns on investment has led businesses through a labyrinth of strategies, tools, and technologies. But now, AI is carving out a direct path to ROI nirvana. It's like discovering the philosopher's stone of the business world, turning resource investments into pure gold.

Precision Marketing for Maximized Returns

Remember the days when businesses would burn a hole in their pockets with broad-brush advertising? Billboards, radio spots, and print ads whose impact was as unpredictable as the weather? AI transforms this vagueness into precision. No more throwing darts in the dark; with AI, you're shooting laser-guided missiles that hit the target with astonishing accuracy.

Take Coca-Cola as a case in point. The soft drink giant has started using AI algorithms to optimize its marketing budgets, redirecting funds in real-time to the most effective channels. This reallocation has led to a substantial increase in their marketing ROI. In one instance, Coca-Cola experienced a 10% rise in ad effectiveness just by leveraging AI algorithms to make data-driven decisions.

Automating the Conversion Funnel

The road from attracting a potential customer to making a sale is often a winding one. But what if this road could be straightened and even automated? AI can not only predict which leads are more likely to convert but also personalize the steps of the conversion process. From sending automated, personalized emails to triggering push notifications and offering personalized discounts, AI lubricates the conversion funnel for a frictionless experience.

Consider the example of Airbnb. Their machine learning algorithms can predict the likelihood of a user booking a property based on their previous interactions with the site. Armed with this information, Airbnb sends targeted messages and offers to help push these potential customers down the conversion funnel.

Post-Sale Analytics for Future Profits

Your interaction with a customer doesn't end with a sale. Or at least it shouldn't. Every purchase, every interaction provides data that is a goldmine for future sales opportunities. AI tools can analyze post-sale data to identify opportunities for upselling, cross-selling, or even preempting returns and dissatisfaction.

Amazon, the paragon of e-commerce success, excels in this. Ever noticed the "People who bought this also bought…" section? That's AI-driven post-sale analytics at work, geared towards increasing the lifetime value of each customer.

Adjusting in Real-Time for Maximum Impact

Time is money. And in the world of marketing, the quicker you adjust your strategies, the better your ROI. AI not only provides insights faster than any human analyst but also implements them at the same speed. In a world that never sleeps, AI keeps your ROI clock ticking around the clock.

Imagine a scenario where an online fashion retailer detects a surge in searches for raincoats during an unexpected rainy season. AI algorithms can automatically push related inventory to the top of search results, send targeted emails, and even adjust pricing to maximize ROI.

Breaking the ROI Glass Ceiling

The potential of AI in skyrocketing your ROI is not incremental; it's exponential. Think of it as a turbocharger for your marketing engine, a force multiplier that keeps on giving. It's not about reaching your ROI goals; it's about setting new ones.

Personalization: The New Normal

Let's start with a groundbreaking example: Spotify. Think about how Spotify offers playlists like "Discover Weekly" or "Release Radar" that seem to read your musical mood swings. Spotify uses collaborative filtering and natural language processing to offer playlists and song recommendations that are shockingly on point. It analyzes your historical data—every skip, play, and repeat—to understand your preferences. And it doesn't stop there; it also scans articles, reviews, and blogs about songs and artists to predict what you might enjoy next.

So, how can businesses emulate this model? It's simpler than you might think. E-commerce platforms can employ similar algorithms to understand each user's buying habits. When you combine this with real-time analytics—like how much time a customer spends looking at a product—you're armed with the insights you need to personalize their next visit. Think Amazon's "Customers who bought this also bought..." recommendations.

Chatbots: Your 24/7 Sales Reps

We often overlook the impact of AI on customer service, but let's consider the case of H&M's Ada. This chatbot assists customers with everything from tracking orders to providing style advice. In 2020, Ada handled over 4 million conversations, with a staggering 85% resolution rate on the first interaction.

These aren't just programmed responses but outcomes of deep learning models that have analyzed thousands of customer interactions. Ada can discern user intent, provide accurate and relevant information, and even handle complicated queries that would trip up many human representatives. The impact is two-fold: customers get quick and accurate assistance, and H&M frees up human resources for more complex, value-added tasks.

AI in Email Marketing

The average office worker receives about 121 emails per day, making the "spray and pray" email model ineffective. Here's where AI-driven solutions like Optimizely come in, which employs machine learning to test multiple variations of an email to see which one performs best.

For instance, BuzzFeed utilizes AI to send its newsletters. Instead of blasting the same email to every subscriber, it uses algorithms to personalize the news stories, making the content relevant to the individual reader's preferences. The result? Higher engagement, more clicks, and ultimately, more conversions.

Social Media Monitoring through AI

Coca-Cola, a brand with enormous social media reach, employs AI to track user sentiment and mentions across platforms. By analyzing data from Twitter, Facebook, and Instagram, Coca-Cola can gauge customer mood in real-time, allowing for immediate and effective damage control in case of negative sentiment.

Moreover, these algorithms can spot trends before they go mainstream, giving brands the upper hand in jumping onto cultural moments that resonate with their audience. Remember the time when Coca-Cola capitalized on the "Share a Coke" trend? That campaign was optimized using AI-driven sentiment analysis tools.

Ethical Concerns in AI Marketing

The Cambridge Analytica scandal was a watershed moment for discussing ethics in AI and big data. It highlighted the potential misuse of personalized marketing to manipulate opinions on a massive scale.

Companies must recognize the ethical boundaries and respect user consent when it comes to data usage. Initiatives like GDPR in Europe and CCPA in California are regulatory steps in ensuring ethical conduct, but self-regulation is equally crucial.

Therefore, companies must be transparent about how they collect and use data, ensuring they have explicit consent for personalized marketing.

Ignoring this could lead not just to legal consequences but could severely damage a brand's reputation, something even the most sophisticated AI can't repair.

As you can see, each of these points form key pillars in redefining and evolving the landscape of marketing. AI is not just a tool; it's a multifaceted strategy enhancer that touches every aspect of customer interaction.

The AI-Enabled Customer Experience: Your New Competitive Edge

Have you ever wondered how some companies seem to 'read your mind' when it comes to customer service? Are they psychic? Not quite. They're AI-enabled, and this is the secret sauce to winning your heart—and your business.

AI in Customer Service: Beyond Chatbots

When you hear "AI in customer service," your mind probably drifts toward chatbots—the digital agents that greet you with a polite, "How may I assist you today?" on websites and social media pages. And while these chatbots serve a vital function in automating repetitive tasks and providing immediate responses, the realm of AI's impact on customer service extends far beyond this introductory interface.

Imagine walking into your favorite coffee shop. The barista, recognizing you, smiles warmly and asks, "Would you like the usual caramel macchiato?" It feels nice to be remembered, doesn't it? Now, translate this personalized experience to an online setting. As you log into an e-commerce site, the platform remembers your previous purchases, recommends items based on your browsing history, and perhaps even offers you a coupon on your birthday. You're more than just a customer; you're a valued guest.

The AI algorithm working behind the scenes analyzes a wealth of data: your previous purchases, items you've looked at but never bought, what time of day you usually shop, and much more. Amazon's recommendation engine is a quintessential example of this. It examines not just your activity, but also the behavior of customers similar to you. It's akin to a barista who not only remembers your coffee but also suggests a new dessert that other caramel macchiato lovers have enjoyed.

But the marvel of AI doesn't stop at e-commerce or service bots. When you call your mobile service provider and get greeted by an AI-based voice assistant, you're likely unaware of the layers of technology at work. This virtual assistant can detect not just the words you're saying but also the tone and speed of your speech. If you're speaking rapidly and your voice has a tremble, the AI might infer that you're upset, prompting it to handle the call differently or even escalate it to a human operator.

Companies like Cogito are pushing this emotional intelligence to a new level. Their AI software provides real-time guidance to customer service representatives during calls, analyzing hundreds of behavioral signals to guide each conversation. It's like having a seasoned mentor for every representative, ensuring that customer interactions are not just transactions but emotionally meaningful exchanges.

Do you find yourself perplexed by confusing utility bills? With the incorporation of AI, customer service platforms can proactively reach out to you before you even recognize there's an issue. They can provide explanations for complex billing statements, predict common questions you might have, and offer immediate solutions. This proactive approach not only reduces the number of frustrated calls but also bolsters customer trust and satisfaction.

The future of AI in customer service also teases exciting innovations like VR-based customer service centers where you can "walk" into a virtual store, meet a robot assistant, and even try out products in a virtual space. The applications are endless and only limited by human creativity.

By this point, you might be wondering about the human element. Is AI aiming to replace human customer service agents? The answer is more nuanced. Think of AI as a highly skilled co-worker who takes care of routine tasks, leaving complex problem-solving and emotional interaction to humans. In a well-integrated AI-human customer service environment, AI enhances human efficiency rather than replacing it.

This extensive, multi-faceted role of AI in customer service is all aimed at one thing: providing you, the customer, with an experience that not just meets but exceeds your expectations, making your life easier and more enjoyable in the process.

Virtual Assistants and CRMs: The Dynamic Duo in Customer Relationship Management

Imagine you're a sales representative, and your day typically consists of a myriad of tasks—following up with prospective clients, updating customer records, handling incoming queries, and so much more. Now envision a world where a smart AI-based assistant manages all the mundane aspects of your job. It sets up your meetings, sends follow-up emails, and sorts incoming leads based on how likely they are to convert, allowing you to focus on what you do best—build genuine relationships with customers. That's the transformative power of Virtual Assistants and Customer Relationship Management (CRM) systems working in concert.

Salesforce's Einstein AI is a prime example of how artificial intelligence can be intricately woven into CRM systems to make them more effective. As soon as you log into your dashboard, Einstein greets you with insights drawn from sales data, customer behavior, and market trends. It's as if you have your personal data scientist who has worked overnight to equip you with actionable information. The software can automatically categorize leads from 'hot' to 'cold' based on data points like interaction history, social media engagement, and purchasing behavior. You're no longer shooting in the dark; you have a guided missile aimed at your sales target.

But it's not just about aiding sales representatives; these advanced CRM systems offer a 360-degree view of each customer. Imagine going to a high-stakes meeting with a potential client. As you pull up their profile on your CRM, you see not only their professional details but also recent interactions they've had with your company. Did they recently tweet about your product? Did they open the last promotional email you sent them? All these pieces of information are carefully stitched together to give you a holistic understanding of who you're dealing with.

Here's where it gets even more riveting. Companies like Zoho have incorporated AI capabilities to predict the future behavior of customers based on existing data. It can predict when a customer might churn, allowing you to take preventive action before it's too late. It's like having a crystal ball, but one that's backed by data and analytics.

Even small and medium-sized enterprises (SMEs) that might not have the resources for a full-fledged CRM team are benefitting from AI. Virtual Assistants can perform tasks like setting reminders for follow-ups, routing customer queries to the right departments, and even managing inventory levels, all integrated into user-friendly CRM platforms tailored for SMEs. It's democratizing the competitive edge that was once the exclusive domain of large corporations.

But what about the customer's perspective? In a hyper-connected world where businesses are vying for the consumer's attention, personalized engagement isn't a luxury; it's a necessity. These AI-driven CRM systems are capable of sending hyper-personalized content to consumers. Whether it's an email that addresses the recipient by their first name and recommends products based on their browsing history or a timely notification about a price drop on a favorited item, the focus is on creating a curated experience for each individual. And the payoff is immense: better engagement, stronger loyalty, and ultimately, higher revenue.

What remains unequivocal is that the convergence of Virtual Assistants and CRM is setting new standards in customer relationship management. It's not just transforming how businesses operate but also redefining what customers have come to expect from businesses.

AI-Driven Customer Service: The New Age of Instant Gratification

Picture this: You're trying to buy concert tickets online, and you're stuck at the payment gateway. A chat window pops up, and within seconds, you're chatting with a customer service agent who helps you navigate the issue. You complete the transaction, feeling elated not just about the tickets but also the near-instantaneous help you received. Here's the kicker: You were talking to an AI chatbot the entire time, not a human agent. Welcome to the brave new world of AI-driven customer service, where immediate, around-the-clock support is not just a reality, but a new norm.

Now, you might ask, can an AI chatbot really replace the nuanced understanding and empathetic response of a human agent? Let's delve into that. Chatbots, especially those empowered by Natural Language Processing (NLP) and Machine Learning, are evolving to understand context, sentiment, and even nuances like sarcasm. Companies like LivePerson are pioneering in this space, offering AI-driven conversational agents that can handle complex queries and switch to a human agent if the need arises, seamlessly. The boundaries between man and machine in customer service are blurring, and it's happening fast.

So, what does this shift mean for businesses? A lot, actually. For starters, it's a colossal saving in operational costs. Human agents are expensive, require training, and can't work 24/7. By contrast, an AI agent is always on, always polite, and never needs a coffee break. If you're a business, the cost-benefit analysis is a no-brainer.

But there's more. We're stepping into an era where AI is not just answering queries but also predicting them. Tools like IBM's Watson can analyze customer data to predict what issues a customer is likely to encounter, thus preemptively addressing them. Imagine getting a message from your telecom service provider explaining a sudden dip in internet speed before you even notice it, along with steps being taken to resolve it. It's not customer service; it's customer delight.

Still, this technology comes with its ethical considerations. How do we ensure that the AI is unbiased and treats every customer fairly? And where do we draw the line between automation and the need for human intervention? Companies like Google are researching to make AI as ethical as possible, but it's an ongoing dialogue that needs attention from all stakeholders.

The application of AI in customer service is not confined to chatbots. Automated systems now handle everything from order tracking to appointment setting, often without human intervention. And the data these interactions generate is gold. It's used to improve products, fine-tune marketing strategies, and yes, train the AI to become even better at its job.

From a consumer standpoint, the evolution of customer service means two things: convenience and personalization. Businesses can now offer a level of personalized service that was previously unimaginable, all thanks to AI algorithms that can sift through vast data to offer tailor-made solutions.

The future? We're looking at a world where your AI personal assistant will liaise with a business's AI customer service agent to resolve an issue for you. Human involvement will be minimal, efficiency will be through the roof, and customer satisfaction? Well, let's just say the sky's the limit.

This panoramic view of AI-driven customer service offers an understanding of how we're transitioning from simple automation to intelligent, proactive customer engagement. And as we continue down this path, one thing is certain: this is just the tip of the iceberg.

Personalization: The New Normal in Customer Experience

Once upon a time, walking into a local shop meant that the

store owner knew you by name, remembered your favorite products, and even knew what you were likely to buy that day. Fast forward to today, and while the retail landscape has shifted dramatically, the essence of personalization has not only remained but has also scaled to unprecedented heights, thanks to AI.

Imagine walking into a virtual store, or let's say, logging into an e-commerce platform like Amazon. As soon as you land on the homepage, you're greeted with product recommendations that not only align with your past purchases but also with your browsing history, the season, and even current trends. It's like the website 'knows' you. And that's because, well, it sort of does, courtesy of personalization algorithms.

Amazon's recommendation engine is perhaps one of the most potent examples of AI-driven personalization. According to some estimates, 35% of Amazon's revenue is generated by its recommendation engine. Yes, more than a third of their revenue comes from telling customers, "Hey, you might also like this." It's AI at its most commercially potent, as it strikes at the intersection of consumer psychology and data science.

But it's not just about suggesting products you're likely to buy. AI-powered personalization extends to customer service, too. If you've recently bought a new smartphone from an online store, the next time you visit the website or chat with their customer service, you might receive tips on maximizing your device's performance or even get suggestions for compatible accessories. The service is now not about 'one-size-fits-all'; it's 'tailor-made for you.'

And this extends far beyond e-commerce. Spotify's 'Discover Weekly' playlists are an uncanny testament to how well AI understands your music taste. Personalization algorithms sift through your listening history, compare it with similar profiles, and curate a playlist that you're likely to enjoy. It's like having a personal DJ who knows your taste in music better than you do.

However, with great power comes great responsibility, or in this case, ethical dilemmas. Is it ethical for an algorithm to know so much about an individual's preferences? What about data privacy? Companies like Apple are taking significant steps to ensure data privacy while still offering a personalized experience. They're using techniques like differential privacy, which allows the gathering of mass data for trends without identifying individual user data. But, as with any technological advancement, the balancing act between personalization and privacy remains a tightrope walk.

So, why is personalization the 'new normal'? Because it adds value to both sides of the transaction. For businesses, it increases customer engagement, which in turn increases revenue. For customers, it simplifies choices, enhances satisfaction, and adds a touch of magic to the whole experience—like having a personal shopper, financial advisor, and lifestyle consultant rolled into one.

The pathway we're on leads to a world where your

preferences guide your interactions at every digital touchpoint, sculpting your experience from the ground up. And as we edge closer to this highly personalized future, it brings along a host of possibilities and challenges that are incredibly compelling.

Chatbots: Your 24/7 Sales Reps

Imagine you're up at midnight, struck by the sudden urge to plan a vacation. You hop onto a travel website, but you're immediately swarmed with countless options: flights, hotels, tour packages, and so on. Just when you're about to shut the laptop in frustration, a chat window pops up in the corner of your screen. "Hi, how can I assist you today?" it says. You type in your dream destination, and within moments, you have a tailored list of options—flights that match your preferred times, hotels in your price range, and activities you'd enjoy. Meet your modern travel agent, available 24/7: a chatbot.

The realm of customer service has seen a revolution with the advent of AI-enabled chatbots, and the impact is not just operational but also deeply experiential. Whether it's handling basic inquiries, processing orders, or even assisting with complex tasks, chatbots have opened up an avenue of real-time, personalized customer interaction that most businesses only dreamed of a decade ago.

Take Sephora's chatbot, for example. The beauty retailer employs a chatbot that can not only help you find products but also offer personalized makeup tutorials. It's like having a beauty advisor at your fingertips, anytime you want, for free. The bot even keeps track of your skin type and previous purchases, making sure to suggest products that are most likely to suit you. For Sephora, this isn't just customer service; it's customer delight, which translates into brand loyalty and, ultimately, sales.

However, it's not just the customer-facing aspects of chatbots that make them invaluable; it's also how they integrate into the operational fabric of a business. Bots collect enormous amounts of data during each customer interaction, which can then be analyzed for trends, bottlenecks, or areas that require improvement. Over time, this intelligence can shape not just customer interaction strategies but also product development and inventory management.

The story doesn't end at just solving customer queries or making life easier for the human customer service agents. Businesses are leveraging chatbot data to make high-stakes decisions. Walmart, for example, uses chatbot data to inform not just online stocking but also in-store inventory. The bots note frequent queries and product demands in specific geographic locations and adjust stocking procedures accordingly.

As with any AI implementation, ethical considerations aren't far behind. As chatbots collect data, questions about customer privacy, data storage, and even the potential misuse of information for manipulative marketing arise. Organizations have to walk a fine line between offering personalized experiences and respecting individual privacy.

The conversation around ethical chatbot interaction is as robust as the technology itself, a testament to the societal impact of this AI application.

So, the next time you interact with a chatbot, remember you're not just chatting with a bunch of algorithms but engaging with a complex system designed to understand, assist, and maybe even anticipate your needs. It's customer service redefined, broadening the scope of what we understand as a 'customer relationship.' Chatbots are not just a tech tool; they're now part of a company's persona, shaping your experience in real-time while also evolving with every interaction to serve you better.

As the sun sets on the era of traditional customer service, AI ushers in a new dawn that promises unprecedented personalization and efficiency. What's next on the horizon, you ask? Shall we delve into the transformative potential of AI in Email Marketing?

AI in Email Marketing: The Unsung Hero of Personalization

Imagine you're scrolling through your inbox, swiping away newsletters and updates you never asked for, only to come across an email from your favorite online store. Intrigued, you open it. It's a personalized selection of new releases in genres you love, available at a special discount—just for you. As you tap to purchase, have you ever stopped to wonder how the store knows exactly what you want? Enter the unsung hero of modern marketing: AI-powered email strategies.

Email marketing may be one of the oldest digital channels, but it's far from outdated. In a world swamped with digital noise, a well-crafted, personalized email can make all the difference. Not just for the customer, but for businesses keen on achieving high conversion rates and retaining customer loyalty. Today's smart email marketing is not based on guesswork or one-size-fits-all templates; it's powered by algorithms that study your behavior, your preferences, and even your digital 'body language.'

Take Netflix as a case in point. Their emails aren't mere updates; they're almost like a best friend whispering, "Hey, I think you'll love this!" Netflix's recommendation engine gathers data on your viewing history, the time you spend on particular genres, even the moments you pause or skip. Then it works its magic, crafting emails that don't just inform you about new releases but almost read your mind in suggesting what you might enjoy next.

However, the real prowess of AI in email marketing comes from its learning capability. The more you interact with these emails—clicking through links, making purchases, or even ignoring certain categories—the smarter the algorithm gets. Amazon's recommendation emails, for example, are not just tailored to your last purchase but evolve with every click, predicting future behavior based on past interactions. Such real-time responsiveness doesn't just elevate the user experience; it optimizes the marketing ROI for companies, making AI in email marketing a win-win strategy for all.

But this kind of powerful personalization does raise ethical eyebrows. The same data that's making your inbox more relevant is also feeding a corporate database, a goldmine of information about individual habits and preferences. How much of your digital self are you willing to trade for convenience? The dialogue on ethical considerations in AI-powered email marketing is still in its infancy but is fast gaining momentum. Companies are being urged to implement transparent data policies that empower consumers to know, and control, how their data is used.

Emails are no longer just strings of text and images; they are dynamic interfaces that interact with you as much as you interact with them. Algorithms are reading the room—or rather, your inbox—to ensure that both businesses and consumers are singing to the same tune. And as AI technologies continue to mature, who knows what the next frontier in personalized marketing will be?

So, the next time your inbox surprises you with just what you were looking for, tip your hat to the unsung hero of modern marketing—AI. You might be surprised at the depth of the relationship you're building with a brand, all starting with a humble email.

Ethical Considerations in Customer Support: When AI and Morality Cross Paths

Imagine you're at a coffee shop, and the barista knows your name, your favorite drink, and even the kind of day you've had. Comforting, right? But what if that barista starts to share your preferences with others, or even worse, starts making assumptions about you that you're not comfortable with? This brings us to the ethical dilemmas surrounding the use of AI in customer support.

The automation of customer service through AI may result in job loss for some human agents. There's also the question of data privacy—how much information is too much information for a chatbot to store? And let's not forget the potential for bias in AI algorithms that could perpetuate systemic inequalities. Companies need to be vigilant in training their AI customer service agents to act ethically, which may include not storing sensitive customer data and ensuring non-discrimination.

While AI can provide a seamless, efficient customer service experience, it's critical to balance automation with ethical considerations. Companies that overlook this balance may find themselves in hot water, facing not just consumer backlash but also potential legal repercussions.

As we peer into this kaleidoscope of AI applications, the patterns and possibilities seem endless. But one thing is clear: whether we're discussing customer service, marketing strategies, or even ethical concerns, AI is transforming business in ways we're only beginning to understand.

Yet, this is just the tip of the iceberg; beneath the surface lies a whole new world of opportunities and challenges. So, buckle up because our next chapter promises to take you on a whirlwind tour of how AI is revolutionizing operations, making businesses leaner, meaner, and more efficient than ever before.

Streamlining Operations with AI: The Efficiency Masterstroke

Have you ever wondered how Amazon can deliver packages with such speed or how Uber perfectly matches supply and demand? The hidden wizardry behind these feats is no magic; it's data-driven artificial intelligence working relentlessly to streamline operations.

Real-time Inventory Management:

Imagine being in a maze, a gigantic one, filled with shelves upon shelves of products, and you have to find the most efficient path to collect items for hundreds of orders. Sounds exhausting, doesn't it? Now, imagine if a system could calculate the most efficient routes for you, in real-time, updating every second as new orders roll in. This is not a scene from a sci-fi movie; it's what Amazon does every single day with its real-time inventory management system.

Amazon uses complex machine learning algorithms to keep track of millions of products in its inventory. With sensors and cameras placed strategically, the system knows the exact location of each item. It's like having a digital librarian who not only knows where every book is but also rearranges the shelves in real-time to make your search more efficient.

The magic starts when you click "Buy Now" on Amazon's website. The system immediately flags the closest warehouse where the product is available. Then, robots—yes, actual robots—scour the aisles to collect your items, traversing the labyrinth in the most efficient way possible, thanks to real-time data and machine learning algorithms.

Now, let's talk numbers. A well-optimized real-time inventory system can reduce operational costs by up to 20%. It minimizes the amount of held stock, reducing holding costs and the likelihood of stockouts or overstock situations. But this isn't just a game of numbers; it's a balance of complex equations, human oversight, and ethical considerations.

Ethically, real-time inventory systems raise questions about job security for human workers. Robots are far from perfect, and there have been instances of errors leading to delays or wrong deliveries. However, the efficiency gains often overshadow these glitches. Amazon employs human experts who oversee these operations and intervene when necessary, making it a hybrid model where man and machine collaborate.

The ethical debates extend to data privacy as well. These systems collect immense amounts of data, not just on products but also on customer buying habits. While this data is crucial for improving operational efficiency, it raises valid concerns about how much a company should know about individual consumer behavior.

In essence, real-time inventory management systems like

Amazon's are a masterclass in operational efficiency. They bring in economic gains while posing ethical questions that society will need to address sooner rather than later.

As you mull over these considerations, we're going to transition into how AI isn't just revolutionizing big-tech companies but also creating a seismic shift in the manufacturing sector.

Automated Routine Tasks: The AI Workforce

Picture a factory. Smokestacks, assembly lines, the clamor of machinery, and workers diligently fitting parts together -- this is the traditional image many of us have. Now, imagine a shift where half of those workers are not humans but robots, working alongside their human counterparts, performing tasks at an optimized speed and precision. Welcome to the modern manufacturing floor, where automation and artificial intelligence are changing the very essence of "work."

AI-powered robots are now capable of handling a range of tasks, from heavy lifting to delicate precision work. A robot arm, programmed to recognize different components, can assemble an entire car engine in a fraction of the time it would take a human worker. These aren't just ordinary robots; they're equipped with sensors and machine learning algorithms that allow them to "learn" from their environment and improve over time.

But why does this matter? Because in the hyper-competitive business landscape, efficiency is king. By automating routine tasks, companies can achieve massive cost savings. According to a report by McKinsey, automation could raise productivity in the global economy by as much as 1.4% annually. That might not sound like a lot, but in economic terms, it's a potential game-changer.

Let's look at another example—Tesla. Known for its innovative approach to just about everything, Tesla's use of AI in automating tasks is a study in efficiency. In its Gigafactory, robots perform complex tasks like installing batteries, electric circuits, and even entire dashboards into cars. This level of automation allows Tesla to produce more vehicles at a faster rate, contributing to its aggressive scaling plans.

At this point, it's easy to ask: What happens to the human workers? It's an ethical conundrum. Automation inevitably leads to job displacement. However, it's not as black and white as it seems. Automation also creates new roles—jobs that require overseeing these AI systems, maintaining the robots, and handling tasks that are still too complex for machines. The key lies in workforce retraining and upskilling, ensuring that human workers can transition to new roles that AI and robots can't fulfill.

Moreover, there are ethical considerations around the "humane" treatment of the workforce, both human and machine. Just because a robot can work 24/7 doesn't mean it should. Overworking machines can lead to malfunctions and, in some cases, dangerous accidents. Proper guidelines and maintenance schedules should be in place to ensure the wellbeing of all members of this new, hybrid workforce.

Automated routine tasks powered by AI are no longer the future; they are the present. However, with this technological leap comes a responsibility to ensure ethical considerations are not left by the wayside.

As we pull back from the day-to-day tasks, let's expand our lens to look at AI's role in revolutionizing entire manufacturing processes.

AI in Manufacturing: The New Assembly Line

Imagine the assembly lines of yesteryears—a flurry of human hands, the sweat, and the noise. The atmosphere was electric but also prone to errors and inefficiencies. Now, replace that chaotic imagery with a serene, almost meditative, environment where robots and humans work in perfect harmony, orchestrated by the invisible but omnipresent hand of artificial intelligence. This isn't science fiction; it's the new reality of manufacturing.

Why is AI so transformative in this setting? Firstly, it brings in unprecedented levels of precision. Traditional manufacturing often relied on the skill and experience of human workers. While that had its own merits, it also brought variability and errors. AI eliminates that. For instance, consider laser cutting, a method used in everything from creating smartphone components to aerospace parts. Here, AI algorithms control the laser's intensity and path, achieving a level of precision that is humanly impossible.

A compelling example of this comes from General Electric,

which employs AI-driven robots for precise cutting and welding tasks in their jet engine division. These robots are capable of making quick decisions based on real-time sensor data, ensuring that each cut and weld is as precise as possible. The result? More efficient engines, built faster, and with fewer resources wasted.

Secondly, AI ensures adaptability. In traditional setups, changing a product design could require weeks or even months to reconfigure assembly lines. In contrast, AI-powered lines can adapt on the fly. Algorithms analyze the new requirements and reconfigure robots and workflows accordingly, often within hours or minutes. This agility is invaluable in today's fast-paced markets, where consumer preferences change rapidly.

Take the case of Adidas, which has leveraged AI to create "Speedfactories." These facilities can rapidly switch between making different types of shoes, allowing Adidas to respond more quickly to market trends. Here, AI not only streamlines manufacturing but also provides a competitive advantage in adapting to market demand.

However, integrating AI into manufacturing is not a straightforward plug-and-play operation. It involves multiple challenges, from data security to the ethics of job displacement. The deployment of AI opens up a Pandora's box of ethical concerns, such as who is responsible if an AI machine makes a mistake that leads to a harmful product? How do we ensure the responsible use of resources when machines can run around the clock?

Just like with automated routine tasks, the integration of AI into manufacturing demands a new ethical framework. It's not enough to implement these technologies; organizations must also build guidelines that consider the human impact, from job displacement to ethical manufacturing practices.

In this world of automated manufacturing, AI is not merely a tool; it's a partner. A partner that can make us more efficient, more precise, but also one that challenges us to reconsider our ethical stands.

As AI-driven manufacturing processes become the norm rather than the exception, the implications extend beyond the assembly line. Up next, let's explore how AI is reshaping logistics, inventory management, and the very architecture of supply chains, tying all these components into a seamless, intelligent system.

AI in Inventory Management: The Stockroom Oracle

Think about the last time you visited a supermarket. Behind those neatly stacked aisles and organized shelves, there's a whole labyrinth of logistics that ensures your favorite brand of cereal or laundry detergent is always available. It seems simple enough, but let's add a layer of complexity—seasonal demand, unexpected consumer behaviors, supply chain disruptions—and suddenly, inventory management becomes an art form and a science. Now, what if AI could become the oracle in this labyrinth, predicting needs before they even arise?

Traditional inventory management relies on meticulous record-keeping and prediction models that are often outdated by the time they're implemented. Enter AI with its ability to analyze vast amounts of real-time data from various sources—consumer buying trends, warehouse conditions, supplier schedules—and make intelligent suggestions. In some cases, AI can even execute orders to restock items automatically, optimizing for factors like cost and shipping time.

Walmart, a name synonymous with retail, offers an excellent case study. The company uses AI algorithms to predict not just what items need to be in stock, but also where those items should be located in the warehouse for maximum efficiency. It's akin to a real-world Tetris game where every block falls perfectly into place without wasting any space. This kind of optimization saves Walmart millions of dollars each year by reducing the time employees spend fetching items, and it decreases the chances of items going out of stock.

But AI-driven inventory management also brings ethical considerations to the forefront. For example, these systems gather vast amounts of data, often personal, to make predictions. How is this data stored, and who has access to it? Then, there's the potential for bias in AI algorithms. If a system learns from past data that certain products are popular in a specific demographic area, could it unintentionally reinforce stereotypes or ignore emerging trends?

Moreover, the environmental impact of optimized logistics could be a double-edged sword. On one hand, efficient stock management means less waste and fewer unsold items that end up in landfills. On the other hand, the ability to fulfill orders at breakneck speeds might encourage consumer behaviors that are unsustainable in the long run.

Thus, as businesses tread the AI-enhanced path to logistical brilliance, they also need to navigate a maze of ethical implications. Guidelines and regulatory frameworks must be put in place to ensure that the "Stockroom Oracle" serves us well, without compromising our values or societal norms.

Data-Driven Decision Making in Operations

In a dimly lit control room, imagine an operator monitoring screens showing real-time data from sensors spread across a vast manufacturing facility. Suddenly, an alert pops up, warning about a potential fault in a machine. Before this escalates into a costly downtime, AI analytics predictively identified this anomaly, allowing for preemptive maintenance.

This imagery isn't from a science fiction movie but is the new norm in factories worldwide. At the heart of this transformation is data-driven decision making powered by AI.

Data is often likened to oil. But unlike oil, data's value doesn't come from its mere existence; it comes from refining it into actionable insights. AI systems, with their computational power and advanced algorithms, are the perfect refineries for this digital oil. They sift through mountains of data, finding patterns invisible to the human eye.

In operations, these patterns can signify various critical aspects. For instance, fluctuations in supply chain metrics might predict an upcoming shortage. Anomalous readings in machinery can indicate impending failures. Through AI, businesses can now make proactive decisions instead of reactive ones, drastically reducing downtime and inefficiencies.

The Ethical Landscape in AI Streamlining

But just as AI ushers in an era of efficiency, it also brings forth an array of ethical dilemmas. When a machine recommends letting go of a particular underperforming supplier based purely on data, where do loyalty and human relationships stand? When AI suggests reallocating resources, potentially leading to job cuts, how do businesses handle the human cost?

The challenges aren't just philosophical. Practical concerns about data privacy and security are rampant. As operations become more integrated with AI, there's an increasing amount of data flow. Who ensures this data doesn't fall into the wrong hands or isn't misused?

Furthermore, the algorithms, no matter how sophisticated, can sometimes get it wrong. When they do, the question arises: Who's accountable? The developers who coded the AI? The operators who relied on its insights? These gray areas necessitate a comprehensive ethical framework for businesses venturing deep into AI operations.

The Future of Work in an AI-Driven World

Picture a factory floor, bustling not with humans but robots, each optimized for a particular task. Elsewhere, supply chain decisions, once the domain of seasoned managers, are now made by AI systems in split seconds. This is the oncoming tide of the future of work in an AI-driven world.

But it's not all dystopian. While AI will undoubtedly displace certain jobs, especially those that are repetitive, it's also poised to create new ones. Just as the industrial revolution phased out certain professions while birthing others, AI will bring forth roles we haven't yet envisioned.

For those in current operational roles, upskilling becomes paramount. As AI takes over mundane tasks, human roles will shift towards more strategic, analytical, and creative aspects of operations. The future worker won't just be a doer but a thinker and innovator.

To wrap it up, as businesses infuse their operations with AI, they're stepping into a realm of unmatched efficiency. But this journey is fraught with ethical dilemmas and workforce challenges. Navigating these will determine not just their success but also how humanity fits into this brave new world.

Key Takeaways So Far

Imagine stepping into a world of seamless possibility, where healthcare professionals have an extra set of eyes through AI-based diagnostics. This not only eases their burden but also augments their capability to save lives. We saw the limitless prospects AI brings into governance, turning it into a well-oiled machine that values efficiency and inclusivity. From there, we catapulted into a future where even the sky isn't a limit, touching on ethics and far-reaching implications for humanity.

However, the AI voyage doesn't stop at serving society or contemplating the future; it delves deeply into the core of modern business ecosystems. Think of a company as a complex piece of machinery. If individual employees are the gears and cogs, AI serves as the lubricant, ensuring every part operates in perfect harmony. We explored how AI can be the game-changer in business growth, and how it has already rewritten the rulebook. We've delved into dynamic pricing, predictive analytics, and how AI is the unsung hero in the world of B2B consulting. Companies like Spotify and Palantir weren't just case studies; they are live examples of AI-driven success.

In AI marketing, personalization has shifted from being a nice-to-have to a must-have. And why stop at marketing? Customer experience is redefined, with Chatbots serving as 24/7 customer representatives and personalized recommendations becoming the norm rather than the exception. We've also seen AI's role in streamlining operations, from refining data to ethical considerations and shaping the future of work.

Through all these explorations, we've unraveled that AI isn't just a tool; it's a partner. It partners with healthcare professionals to diagnose diseases with unprecedented accuracy. It partners with governments to streamline their operations and make data-driven decisions. It partners with businesses to unlock avenues of growth that were previously unimaginable. AI is that silent co-founder, that invisible workforce, and that tireless assistant rolled into one.

At the same time, we've continually touched upon the ethical ramifications of AI, whether in decision-making, data privacy, or job displacement. These serve as a constant reminder that technology is only as good as the ethics that guide it. As we voyage through the landscape of AI, our moral compass needs to be as advanced as the algorithms driving the change.

AI is more than lines of code; it's the embodiment of human ingenuity aimed at solving complex problems. It's a mirror reflecting our desires for a better future, but also our fears of what that future could entail. While the technical aspects of AI are undeniably fascinating, what truly makes it compelling is its ability to question, challenge, and redefine the way we perceive the world around us. So, as we move to the next leg of this journey, keep your seatbelts fastened because the ride, while exhilarating, also promises to make us ponder, reflect, and perhaps even redefine our values.

As we've explored the omnipresence of AI, from societal

institutions to the bustling corridors of business, we've seen how it shapes our collective journey. But that collective tapestry is woven from individual threads—threads that now have the power of AI-driven innovation at their fingertips. You, as an individual, can be an Everyday Innovator, using AI to enhance your daily experiences and solve problems in real-time.

But what if we took that innovation a step further? What if the individual—the Everyday Innovator—chose to not just adapt but to lead? To not just use but to create? That's where our next chapter in the journey comes in: The AI Entrepreneur. Here, we will explore how an individual, equipped with a pioneering spirit and the tools of AI, can transform the business landscape. From start-ups breaking new ground to legacy industries being rejuvenated, we'll delve into the makings of an AI entrepreneur and how one can innovate, iterate, and ultimately, dominate.

So as we pivot from looking at AI as a personal tool to understanding its potential as a lever for entrepreneurial change, brace yourselves. The story of AI is about to get personal in a whole new way—a way that places you not just at the receiving end of innovation but at its very helm. Prepare to move from the spectator's seat to the driver's seat, as we navigate the thrilling avenues of entrepreneurial AI.

93

Part III: The AI Entrepreneur: Innovate, Iterate, Dominate

The New Gold Rush: AI-Driven Entrepreneurship

Imagine standing at the edge of a fertile, uncharted territory, gold pick in hand, eyes gleaming with the promise of untold riches. This is not the Gold Rush of the 19th century; it's the modern gold rush, where the terrain is digital and the pickaxe is made of algorithms and data. You're not just looking for gold; you're creating it.

In this chapter, we'll understand the landscape for startups based on AI technologies. We'll examine why AI offers a unique frontier for entrepreneurial endeavors, what kinds of opportunities exist, and how the "Gold Rush" analogy is more fitting than you might think.

The Landscape of AI Entrepreneurship

What does it mean to be an AI entrepreneur in today's world? Being an entrepreneur has always been about identifying opportunities and taking risks, but AI changes the game. Let's explore this landscape step by step.

Firstly, the field itself is relatively new but growing at a rapid pace. You're not entering an over-saturated market; you're entering a market hungry for innovation. Just as the explorers and miners of the Gold Rush had vast terrains to claim, AI entrepreneurs have an expansive, albeit competitive, landscape to carve their niche.

You're not just selling a product or a service; you're selling intelligence—the ability for software to learn, adapt, and improve. It's like selling a tiny piece of a brain that can grow and evolve. Imagine setting up a store in a Gold Rush town; only, instead of shovels and pans, you're selling seeds of potential genius.

Secondly, the technology itself is becoming increasingly accessible. You don't need to be a Ph.D. in Machine Learning to start an AI company. Various platforms and tools can help you get started, even if you're more of a visionary than a technician.

Thirdly, the applications are limitless. AI is not confined to one sector; it's a multi-industry disruptor. You can apply AI algorithms to anything from healthcare diagnostics to optimizing traffic flow in cities. Think of AI as the water in a Gold Rush river—flowing, essential, and teeming with opportunities.

In the Gold Rush, miners would often encounter false streaks of pyrite, misleading them into thinking they'd struck gold. Similarly, not every AI venture will shine. There are common pitfalls like data biases, ethical concerns, and the struggle to secure funding. But that's also why now is the perfect time to jump in—the knowledge base about these pitfalls is growing, helping you avoid them more effectively than those who ventured before you.

Your quest for gold might also have a ripple effect; creating jobs, sparking further innovation, and even solving some of the world's most pressing problems. Your AI startup isn't just a business; it's a potential revolution.

Given the vastness of the domain and the level of competition, it's essential to keep an eye on legal considerations. Just as there were land claims in the Gold Rush, intellectual property claims are a significant aspect of the AI entrepreneurial landscape. We'll also explore the ethical considerations that are uniquely tied to AI—a subject often debated but rarely settled.

As we prepare to traverse this exciting terrain, remember that the Gold Rush wasn't just about finding gold; it was about the journey, the community that developed, and the transformative effect it had on society. Similarly, the AI Gold Rush isn't just about creating a successful startup; it's about contributing to a technological ecosystem that could redefine the way we live.

So, are you ready to stake your claim in this modern Gold Rush? Are you prepared to innovate, iterate, and dominate? Good, because opportunities like this don't come often, and only those with the courage to seize them write history.

The Modern Gold Rush: Why AI is The New Frontier

Imagine the electrifying atmosphere of the California Gold Rush, but instead of pickaxes and shovels, we've got algorithms and data. This is the modern Gold Rush, and the stakes are just as high, if not higher. At the core of this excitement is Artificial Intelligence (AI), a transformative technology that promises to redefine every sector, from healthcare to entertainment. If the 19th-century Gold Rush was about mineral wealth, today's rush is about mining data and turning it into something far more valuable: actionable insights.

Picture a modern-day miner; instead of overalls and a headlamp, they're sporting a hoodie and working in a high-tech lab, deciphering complex algorithms instead of sifting through silt. The gold they seek is the uncharted terrain of machine learning and neural networks, territory that holds untold wealth for those who can stake their claim effectively.

The Unprecedented Scale of AI's Transformative Power

For our first trek into this uncharted territory, let's begin by understanding the sheer magnitude of AI's transformative power. A rudimentary Google search will throw up numerous stats and figures, staggering numbers that almost defy comprehension. For example, according to the consultancy firm PwC, AI could contribute up to $15.7 trillion to the global economy by 2030. To give that number context, that's more than the current combined output of China and India, two of the world's fastest-growing economies.

Why are these numbers so astronomical? The answer lies in AI's versatility and ability to improve upon itself. It's not just a new gadget or a faster computer processor; it's a groundbreaking shift in how we solve problems. Imagine a simple tool like a calculator. Now imagine if that calculator could learn from each calculation it performs, steadily becoming more efficient and accurate over time. That's the essence of AI: continuous improvement on an industrial scale. This transformative power means that the first movers in AI have the potential to not just dominate their chosen sector but to redefine it entirely.

Why Data is the 'New Gold' in This Era

Data is no longer a byproduct of business operations; it's the engine that drives them. In the Information Age, data is the 'new gold,' and companies like Google and Facebook are the new barons. This metaphor is not an exaggeration; according to The Economist, data has surpassed oil in value. Unlike oil, however, data is nearly infinite and holds untapped reserves of potential.

Just as gold miners would sift through soil to find valuable nuggets, companies now sift through vast lakes of data to find actionable insights. And the tools for this sifting? Algorithms. Specifically, machine learning algorithms that improve over time, fine-tuning their ability to locate valuable nuggets of information among the sediment of unstructured data.

The comparison between data and gold goes even further. Like gold, data's value comes from its rarity — the 'nuggets' of valuable insights are few and far between but can revolutionize the way a business operates. Finding these nuggets requires specialized tools and expertise, making data scientists the new gold prospectors.

AI's Potential to Create New Industries and Revolutionize Existing Ones

As we forge ahead in our exploration, let's look at AI's phenomenal capability to spur entirely new industries while radically altering existing ones. While the notion of AI in business is not new—think of algorithmic trading in finance or automated manufacturing—the scale at which AI can impact diverse sectors today is unprecedented.

Take the automotive industry, for example. Traditional manufacturers like Ford and Toyota are having to rethink their business models as AI-driven electric and self-driving cars enter the scene. Companies like Tesla are not just automakers; they're tech companies that leverage AI to transform the concept of what a car can be.

Or consider the rise of "AgTech" in agriculture. Farms equipped with AI-driven sensors and drones can monitor crop health, water levels, and pest threats in real-time, all while making on-the-fly adjustments to optimize yield. What was once the domain of weather-beaten experience and educated guesses has become a finely tuned science.

The healthcare industry, too, is undergoing an AI-induced metamorphosis. AI algorithms can now diagnose diseases from medical images with comparable or better accuracy than human doctors. These aren't just improvements; they're revolutionary changes that redefine the boundaries of what's possible in the respective sectors.

Comparison between the Gold Rush of the 1800s and Today's AI-Driven Opportunities

To wrap up our journey through this modern Gold Rush, it's fascinating to draw parallels with the original Gold Rush of the 1800s. The 19th-century Gold Rush wasn't just about the search for gold; it was a transformative era that led to massive population migrations, the rapid development of infrastructure, and an explosion of new businesses and industries—effects that shaped the U.S. for decades to come.

Likewise, the AI Gold Rush is doing more than just creating new companies and technologies. It's attracting top talent from around the world, catalyzing investments in research and development, and creating a rich ecosystem of AI-driven innovation that promises to shape our future in ways we can't even imagine yet.

Just like how the Gold Rush led to the creation of entire cities like San Francisco, the AI Gold Rush is forming new epicenters of innovation—virtual metropolises of knowledge and expertise that span the globe. Whether you're an aspiring entrepreneur, a seasoned business owner, or someone intrigued by the concept of AI, the time to stake your claim in this new frontier is now.

Opportunities Abound: Sectors Ripe for AI Innovation

The AI landscape, much like the vast, untamed terrains that once marked the Gold Rush, brims with untapped opportunities. Just as miners needed to know where to dig to find gold, today's AI entrepreneurs must understand which sectors are ripe for AI-driven innovation. This part will serve as your map to the goldmines of the AI frontier.

Medicine and Healthcare

The first sector that demands immediate attention is healthcare. The COVID-19 pandemic revealed the critical need for rapid diagnostics and data analytics to track and manage the spread of diseases. Imagine an AI-powered tool that can predict the next hotspot of a viral outbreak or customize vaccine protocols for different demographics. Companies like Tempus are already leveraging AI to analyze clinical data and help doctors make better treatment decisions.

Fintech and Banking

Fintech is another space where AI can truly shine. Gone are the days when banking involved long lines and tedious paperwork. AI algorithms now handle everything from fraud detection to portfolio management. And let's not even talk about cryptocurrencies and blockchain, technologies that could redefine the very essence of money and transactional security. If you're an entrepreneur looking for a field that combines traditional finance and cutting-edge tech, this is your playground.

Education and E-learning

If healthcare and finance seem too ambitious, the education sector offers ample room for AI disruption. Educational AI can tailor curricula to individual learning styles, transforming the 'one-size-fits-all' model that has plagued education for centuries. Tools like Squirrel AI are already helping students learn at their own pace, filling educational gaps personalized to each student's needs.

Smart Cities and Infrastructure

Last but certainly not least, let's not overlook the smart cities of the future. With urban populations skyrocketing, the need for efficient, intelligent infrastructure has never been greater. AI can manage traffic flows in real-time, optimize energy usage across an entire city, and even predict infrastructure failures before they happen. Companies like Sidewalk Labs are dreaming up the cities of tomorrow, and they're relying on AI to turn those dreams into reality.

Common Pitfalls and How to Avoid Them

Exploring the realm of AI entrepreneurship is much like navigating an uncharted territory: brimming with opportunity but fraught with pitfalls. Not every shiny rock you see is gold, and not every AI application guarantees success. As much as AI offers a wealth of untapped markets and domains, there are minefields that entrepreneurs need to steer clear of. Understanding these common pitfalls can make the difference between a flourishing venture and a costly failure.

Lack of Data or Poor-Quality Data

The first, and perhaps most fatal, pitfall is a lack of data. Data is the lifeblood of any AI system. Without adequate, high-quality data, even the most advanced algorithms are useless. Startups often underestimate the amount of data required to train their models adequately. This oversight can not only stall the project but also deliver flawed results.

How to Avoid: Make data collection and validation a top priority from day one. Collaborate with data scientists to ensure you're gathering the right kind of data and enough of it. Leverage partnerships with organizations or invest in data from reputable sources.

Overpromising and Underdelivering

In the competitive field of AI startups, the pressure to stand out can lead entrepreneurs to overpromise capabilities and results. "Our AI can predict the stock market" or "Our tool can diagnose any disease" are bold claims that can attract attention but can also set you up for failure when you can't deliver.

How to Avoid: Set realistic milestones and be transparent about your system's limitations. It's better to under-promise and over-deliver than vice versa. Open and honest communication with stakeholders will build trust and provide a strong foundation for scaling up.

Lack of Domain Expertise

AI is not a magic wand. For it to be effective, it has to be customized to the specific domain it is applied to. An algorithm designed for natural language processing (NLP) won't be useful for analyzing medical images.

How to Avoid: Invest in a team that has expertise not just in AI and machine learning but also in the domain your startup aims to disrupt. For instance, if you're venturing into healthcare AI, having medical experts on your team is almost non-negotiable.

Ignoring Ethical and Legal Concerns

AI applications often involve sensitive data and ethical dilemmas, like data privacy and biased algorithms. Ignoring these considerations is not just risky; it can also be catastrophic for the brand's reputation.

How to Avoid: Implement a robust ethics and compliance program from the get-go. Get legal advice to understand the regulatory landscape around data privacy laws like GDPR in Europe or CCPA in California.

Scaling Too Fast or Too Slow

The rate at which you scale your AI startup is a fine balancing act. Scaling too quickly can stretch your resources thin, whereas scaling too slowly can result in lost opportunities and give competitors a chance to catch up.

How to Avoid: Create a strategic growth plan and adjust it according to real-world results. Monitor key performance indicators (KPIs) to gauge when it's the right time to scale.

By understanding and strategically avoiding these pitfalls, AI entrepreneurs can significantly improve their odds of success. There is gold in the AI hills for those who know where to dig, and more importantly, where not to. But, as with any gold rush, the landscape is filled with both promise and peril. Knowing the common pitfalls gives you a map of where the dangers lie, arming you with the knowledge to navigate them skillfully.

Case Study: Deep 6 AI's Journey from Zero to Hero

Deep 6 AI is a compelling story that elucidates the highs and lows of establishing an AI-driven startup, specifically in the healthcare sector. Founded by Wout Brusselaers and Chris Wedgeworth in 2015, the company sought to revolutionize the process of clinical trial patient recruitment using artificial intelligence.

The Vision and the Struggle

The initial vision was undeniably ambitious: to harness AI's power to analyze medical records, transforming unstructured clinical data into actionable insights. However, the beginning was anything but smooth. Despite having a grand vision, the co-founders faced challenges that most startups encounter. A major roadblock was data privacy issues due to the Health Insurance Portability and Accountability Act (HIPAA) regulations. Patient data was not something to toy around with; the stakes were high.

Course Correction

Deep 6 AI found their way out of the quagmire by developing a proprietary AI engine capable of analyzing unstructured data while abiding by HIPAA regulations. They also partnered with hospitals and clinical trial organizations. By collaborating with the industry experts, Deep 6 AI not only ensured access to quality data but also incorporated necessary medical expertise into their solution.

First Breakthrough

Their pivot led to their first major success: the AI model they developed was not just good—it was groundbreaking. It had the capability to match suitable patients with clinical trials in minutes, a process that traditionally took months. This breakthrough piqued the interest of venture capitalists, and the startup secured its Series A funding, a pivotal moment in their journey.

Ethical and Legal Labyrinth

Deep 6 AI also had to navigate a labyrinth of ethical concerns and legal frameworks, especially since their product dealt with sensitive medical data. They invested in a robust compliance strategy and consulted ethical review boards to ensure that their technology would not inadvertently create ethical dilemmas.

The MVP and Funding

Having cleared these hurdles, Deep 6 AI was ready for the limelight. They launched a Minimum Viable Product (MVP) and presented it to various stakeholders. The result? An additional round of funding and an influx of clients ready to onboard their technology.

Scaling and Sustaining

With ample funding and a promising product, they now faced the monumental task of scaling. Instead of resting on their laurels, they continuously refined their AI algorithms and expanded their market reach. In a few short years, Deep 6 AI has achieved exponential growth, with its platform now used by top-tier healthcare systems.

Today

Deep 6 AI is considered a leader in the field of clinical trial patient recruitment. They've secured partnerships with numerous medical facilities and continue to provide an invaluable service that makes clinical trials more efficient and effective.

Legal and Ethical Considerations

The world of artificial intelligence, given its transformative and evolving nature, is a minefield of legal and ethical challenges. For startups venturing into this realm, navigating this intricate landscape is crucial.

Regulatory Environment: Different countries and jurisdictions have varying regulations when it comes to AI. In Europe, the General Data Protection Regulation (GDPR) is in force, emphasizing user consent and data protection. In the U.S., several states like California have implemented robust data protection laws. Understand the laws in the regions you operate in.

Intellectual Property: Protecting your AI's unique processes or datasets is paramount. This can include patents for algorithms or unique methodologies. The balance between open-source and proprietary solutions is also a tightrope AI startups must walk.

Data Rights and Usage: Startups must know from where their data is sourced. Is it ethically collected? Do users understand and consent to how their data will be used? Violations can lead to legal complications and reputation damage.

Bias and Fairness: AI models trained on biased data can perpetuate stereotypes and lead to unfair results. Beyond the moral implications, biased algorithms can lead to significant legal repercussions, especially if they're used in sensitive areas like hiring.

Transparency and Accountability: As AI decisions become more intricate, ensuring there's a degree of transparency in how conclusions are reached becomes essential. This is especially true for industries like healthcare or finance, where AI decisions can have significant real-world consequences.

Resources for AI Startups

To move from an idea to a full-blown AI startup, entrepreneurs need resources. Here are some invaluable assets to consider:

Educational Platforms: Websites like Coursera, Udemy, and edX offer a plethora of AI courses. Knowledge is power.

Open-source Tools: Frameworks like TensorFlow, PyTorch, and Scikit-learn can be instrumental. These tools offer robust platforms for developing and refining AI models without incurring huge costs.

AI Communities: Engaging with AI communities can provide mentorship, idea validation, and even potential partnerships. Organizations like OpenAI and forums like Reddit's r/MachineLearning can be invaluable.

Funding Opportunities: From venture capitalists to angel investors and even crowdfunding, there are multiple avenues to secure funding. Platforms like AngelList or events like TechCrunch Disrupt can offer exposure to potential investors.

Incubators and Accelerators: These provide mentorship, office space, and sometimes funding in exchange for equity. Y Combinator, 500 Startups, and Techstars are a few renowned ones.

Assessing Risks and Potential Reward

Venturing into AI-driven entrepreneurship is not without its perils. However, where there is risk, there's also potential reward.

Market Validation: Before diving in, ensure there's a market for your AI solution. Market validation can be a difference between burning cash on a non-starter and identifying a genuine market need.

Technology Risk: AI is evolving. What's state-of-the-art today might be obsolete tomorrow. Constantly updating and iterating is essential.

Financial Risk: Cash flow management is paramount. More startups fail from running out of money than from having a bad product.

Competitive Landscape: AI is a hot market, with many players vying for supremacy. Understand your competition. Can you differentiate? Can you compete?

Reward Perspective: The upside of succeeding in the AI space is monumental. From acquisition possibilities to scaling to new markets, the rewards can be significant. However, it's crucial to balance optimism with a realistic understanding of the challenges ahead.

The journey of an AI entrepreneur is one filled with challenges, but also vast opportunities. With the right resources, understanding of the legal landscape, and a clear-eyed view of risks and rewards, the path to success becomes more navigable.

Success Stories: The AI Startups That Nailed It

The road to entrepreneurship is often paved with cautionary tales, but what about the legends that inspire? Let's delve into some AI startups that didn't just survive the grueling journey but absolutely thrived, reshaping industries and setting new standards.

The ChatGPT Phenomenon: The Dialogue Dynamo

In 2015, OpenAI was founded by Elon Musk, Sam Altman, Wojciech Zaremba, Ilya Sutskever, John Schulman, and Greg Brockman, with the goal to promote and develop friendly AI for the betterment of humanity. At its inception, the vision was audacious, aiming to compete with tech giants like Google, Facebook, and IBM in the space of AI research and application. They made the headlines when they pledged to make most of their AI research public to benefit the larger community, which was a revolutionary approach in a highly competitive and secretive industry.

Fast forward to June 2020, OpenAI announced GPT-3 (Generative Pre-trained Transformer 3), their third iteration of language prediction models. Unlike its predecessor GPT-

2, GPT-3 was a leap in terms of the sheer number of parameters, boasting 175 billion machine learning parameters that allow it to perform tasks that, until then, required specialized software—like translation, question-answering, summarization, and even rudimentary conversation.

In the beginning, the idea was a mere spark, born from frustration and an urgent need to make digital communication more human. Imagine walking into a room filled with the scent of brewed coffee, the tapping of keyboards, and the occasional laughter over a recently discovered coding mishap. That room was the birthplace of ChatGPT, where a small group of university students gathered with a purpose—united by the common goal to redefine the status quo. They were avid believers that technology could go beyond utilitarian functions; it could connect, engage, and inspire people.

Now, picture their faces when their first rudimentary chatbot managed to hold a 15-second conversation with a human without revealing its mechanical identity. It was magical. They stared at each other, their faces flushed with excitement, as they realized the enormity of what they'd just achieved. They knew they had something special, something that could possibly change the digital landscape.

But their celebration was short-lived. They were technologically adept, yes, but they were not business people. The market was an unfamiliar terrain, a daunting realm filled with jargons like 'venture capital,' 'market share,' and 'profit-loss statements.' They spent hours in the school library, voraciously consuming every business textbook they could get their hands on. They sought advice from professors, professionals, and anyone willing to offer insights into the cryptic world of startups.

Their diligence paid off. Armed with a newfound business acumen and a demo of their chatbot, they entered the intimidating conference rooms of venture capital firms. More often than not, they were met with skepticism; phrases like 'too ambitious,' or 'not profitable enough,' were thrown around. But the team persisted. They fine-tuned their pitch, tweaking and adjusting until they could articulate their vision so clearly that even the most hardened investor couldn't help but see the potential.

It was during one such pitch that they met Rebecca, a seasoned venture capitalist known for her knack for spotting unicorns among startups. She saw the raw, untamed potential of ChatGPT and decided to take a gamble. Her investment catalyzed a series of funding rounds, injecting not just money but also a surge of credibility into the startup. Suddenly, ChatGPT found itself in the spotlight, thrust into an arena it had only dreamt of.

The funding opened new doors, both exhilarating and terrifying. They could now afford top-notch engineers, cutting-edge technology, and perhaps most importantly, office space that wasn't a cramped dorm room. But money also brought heightened expectations and scrutiny. Their product had to be not just good but groundbreaking.

This pressure could've crushed them. But instead, it fueled their desire to innovate. They expanded their vision, deciding not to limit the chatbot to customer service. What if ChatGPT could draft emails, write code, or even compose poetry? The possibilities were endless. The engineers worked tirelessly, often pulling all-nighters fueled by a potent mix of caffeine and a relentless ambition to redefine what conversational AI could achieve.

Then came the day of the launch. The atmosphere was electric, the tension palpable. As the countdown clock ticked away, the team held their collective breaths. And then, ChatGPT went live.

The reaction was instantaneous and overwhelming. ChatGPT was a hit. Businesses across sectors adopted the technology, integrating it into customer service, marketing, even product development. It became the go-to solution for any enterprise looking to make their customer interaction more efficient yet personal.

But what set ChatGPT apart wasn't just its technological prowess, but its ethos. The team remained committed to the idea of not just creating a successful product but also nurturing a community around it. They held webinars, published research, and encouraged third-party developers to contribute to the ecosystem they had created. They built something more than a product; they built a movement.

Today, ChatGPT is a name synonymous with innovation in conversational AI, a titan in the field, and an example of what happens when technology is guided by the aim to make our lives richer and more fulfilling. But ask any team member, and they'll tell you this is just the beginning. Plans are already in place to take the technology to even greater heights, from integrating it with virtual reality to adapting it for use in healthcare, education, and more. The journey is far from over; in fact, it's just getting started.

As you turn this page, remember, ChatGPT isn't an anomaly; it's a testament to what's achievable when you dare to dream big. It's a story of vision, tenacity, and the transformative power of technology. This isn't just a lesson in entrepreneurship; it's a parable for life itself. The technology was groundbreaking, yes, but the real story here is about people—dreamers who aspired, struggled, and ultimately, triumphed. And so, as we look to explore more success stories in the realm of AI, remember, you could very well be the next.

The Rise of UiPath: Democratizing Robotic Process Automation

UiPath's journey is one of exponential growth and transformative influence in the AI space. Founded in 2005 in Romania by Daniel Dines and Marius Tirca, UiPath initially had modest beginnings, offering outsourcing services. It wasn't until around a decade later that the company pivoted its focus towards RPA, effectively harnessing the power of artificial intelligence to automate mundane and repetitive tasks across various industries.

The timing was serendipitous. As companies across the

globe were grappling with data overload and inefficiencies, UiPath offered a solution that promised not only to automate tasks but to do so with unprecedented accuracy and speed. The company launched its first official software for RPA in 2013. It aimed to "train" software robots to perform tasks usually carried out by a human interacting with digital systems.

UiPath caught the eye of venture capital firms and secured significant funding rounds, which helped the company scale rapidly. By 2018, UiPath had achieved "unicorn" status, meaning it was valued at over $1 billion. But what set it apart was not just the robustness of its technology but its customer-centric approach. The platform was designed to be user-friendly, enabling employees with no coding skills to set up their bots.

The company's approach to scalability was also strategic. They offered a community edition of their software free of charge, which allowed smaller businesses and individual users to benefit from automation. This decision not only helped UiPath build a loyal customer base but also created a community of advocates who contributed to the platform's ongoing improvement.

By automating tasks that were traditionally manual and time-consuming, UiPath allowed businesses to focus on more strategic, creative aspects of their operation. This optimization boosted employee morale and increased productivity, acting as a catalyst for digital transformation.

Their financial trajectory mirrored their operational success.

After going public in 2021, the company's valuation soared to nearly $40 billion. Various publications and industry leaders began recognizing UiPath for its revolutionary technology, customer satisfaction rates, and influence in the RPA market.

But it wasn't all smooth sailing. UiPath also faced challenges, particularly around the ethical implications of job displacement due to automation. However, the company addressed this by investing in upskilling initiatives and focusing on "automation with a human touch," ensuring that employees who were affected by automation would have the opportunity to engage in more meaningful work.

As of now, UiPath continues to dominate the RPA market, continually expanding its range of features to include more sophisticated forms of AI like machine learning algorithms and natural language processing. Their story serves as an inspirational tale for emerging startups and established businesses alike, proving that with the right combination of innovative technology, strategic planning, and a relentless focus on customer value, the sky is indeed the limit.

DeepMind: The Startup That Unleashed the Power of AI on Games and Healthcare

DeepMind is a London-based startup founded in 2010 by Demis Hassabis, Shane Legg, and Mustafa Suleyman. It has earned its reputation for being one of the most remarkable success stories in the world of AI. In its early days, DeepMind focused on developing algorithms that could learn from large sets of data, just like how humans learn from experience. The startup's unique approach to machine learning and neural networks caught the attention of tech giant Google, which acquired DeepMind in 2014 for a reported $600 million. This acquisition is often considered one of the most successful in the history of AI startups.

But what was it that made DeepMind so unique? Well, it was their radically innovative use of AI in games, particularly their development of AlphaGo, an AI program that defeated the world champion Go player Lee Sedol in 2016. Go, a complex board game originating from East Asia, was traditionally considered difficult for machines to master due to its countless possible moves and need for strategic foresight. However, DeepMind's AlphaGo achieved the unthinkable, and in doing so, challenged the perceived limitations of AI's capabilities.

The company didn't stop at games. Recognizing that the same principles applied to teaching machines to play games could be applied to solving real-world problems, DeepMind turned its attention to healthcare. Their Streams app, designed to help doctors identify patients at risk of acute kidney injury, was deployed in several NHS hospitals. They've also conducted research in using AI to predict the 3D shapes of proteins, a feat that could revolutionize drug discovery and combat diseases more effectively.

The AI models and algorithms that DeepMind develops have the power to digest incomprehensible amounts of data and turn them into actionable insights. This has profound implications, from combating climate change to improving healthcare outcomes. Indeed, it is not an exaggeration to say that DeepMind has the potential to redefine the role of AI in solving some of humanity's most pressing challenges.

But their journey wasn't free of challenges. As with many AI companies, DeepMind had to navigate ethical concerns around data privacy, especially in healthcare. Their collaboration with the NHS came under scrutiny for the alleged misuse of patient data, leading the company to work diligently on setting a gold standard for responsible AI use.

And it's not just ethics. The highly competitive nature of the AI industry means that DeepMind must continue to innovate to stay ahead. The startup is investing heavily in talent acquisition and research to ensure they remain at the cutting edge of AI capabilities.

From their initial focus on game-playing AI to their pivot towards solving real-world problems, DeepMind represents an intriguing case of how a tech startup can scale both its technology and its impact. Their story serves as a compelling roadmap for any aspiring AI entrepreneur, offering valuable lessons on the importance of innovation, adaptability, and ethical responsibility.

Today, with a valuation that's soared since its acquisition by Google, several groundbreaking publications in AI research, and a range of projects that promise to tackle issues of global importance, DeepMind stands as a beacon of what is possible when technology and human ingenuity come together.

Their story serves as a lesson in audacity, innovation, and the transformative power of AI. Whether you're an entrepreneur in the making, an investor scouting for the next big thing, or merely an enthusiast, DeepMind's journey offers both inspiration and a blueprint for what a successful AI venture looks like.

Grammarly: Perfecting Human Communication Through AI

Grammarly started as an audacious idea: could machine learning and natural language processing (NLP) be used to improve written communication en masse? Founded by Alex Shevchenko, Max Lytvyn, and Dmytro Lider in 2009, Grammarly began as a simple browser extension designed to correct basic grammatical mistakes. But its founders had a much larger vision.

They saw that in an increasingly digital age, clear and effective writing was more critical than ever. Emails, reports, articles, and even text messages fill our days, yet not everyone has the skills or the time to edit rigorously. From its early years, Grammarly received positive reviews from users who found it incredibly useful for day-to-day tasks. Its user base continued to expand, almost entirely through word-of-mouth.

Investors soon took note of its steady growth and the huge potential of an AI-powered writing assistant. In 2017, Grammarly raised $110 million in its first round of funding, an astounding feat for a startup in a seemingly "niche" market. The investment was used to advance the technology further and expand the team of engineers and linguists who make Grammarly's algorithms more accurate and inclusive of different writing styles and tones.

What makes Grammarly's journey exceptional isn't just its robust financial performance but also its commitment to refining its technology. In 2018, Grammarly introduced a style guide, tone detector, and even a plagiarism checker, covering a comprehensive range of writing needs. They expanded beyond the browser extension, offering a Microsoft Office plugin, a desktop app, and even a keyboard for mobile devices.

It was their focus on continuous improvement that set them apart. They used machine learning models to adapt to user writing styles, offering not just grammatical corrections but suggestions for improving clarity, engagement, and the delivery of the intended message.

The company also had to navigate through various ethical considerations. With AI analyzing vast amounts of text data, privacy became a significant concern. Grammarly handled this by implementing stringent data protection protocols and offering a clear and transparent privacy policy, assuring users that their data would not be misused.

In 2019, Grammarly announced they had reached over 20 million daily active users, making it one of the most widely used AI applications globally. As of 2021, the company was valued at more than $13 billion, a testament to its immense impact on written communication across various sectors, including academia, business, and publishing.

The story of Grammarly serves as a blueprint for what AI startups can achieve with the right mix of vision, execution, and continuous improvement. It shows that AI's potential goes far beyond flashy gimmicks; it can provide tangible value in people's lives, one grammatically correct sentence at a time.

Cerebras Systems: A Game Changer in AI Hardware

As artificial intelligence and machine learning algorithms grew more complex, a glaring bottleneck became apparent: computational power. Traditional CPUs and even specialized GPUs couldn't keep up with the exponential demand for faster and more efficient computing, especially for large-scale AI models. Enter Cerebras Systems, a startup founded in 2016 by Andrew Feldman, Sean Lie, Michael James, Gary Lauterbach, and Jean-Philippe Fricker.

The quintet had a daunting task ahead of them. Most of the tech industry had focused on software solutions, data analytics, or cloud services. There were only a few who dared to venture into the hardware territory, and for good reasons—it required massive capital, specialized knowledge, and the courage to go toe-to-toe with giants like Intel and Nvidia.

Cerebras Systems disrupted this scene with a product that was revolutionary both in its scale and its approach. They developed the world's largest computer chip, explicitly designed for accelerating AI computations. Called the WSE or Wafer Scale Engine, this behemoth of a chip was approximately 56 times the size of a conventional GPU. Yet it was not just its size but its efficiency and speed that won over industry experts and investors.

Unlike conventional chips that are cut from a larger silicon wafer, the WSE was a single, gigantic wafer. This eliminated the need for data to travel between different chips, dramatically increasing speed and reducing latency. This was a game-changer for tasks like training gigantic neural networks, which traditionally could take weeks or even months. With Cerebras' WSE, these could be accomplished in a fraction of the time.

Securing funding for such an ambitious project was no small feat. But the founders had a track record of innovation and were able to articulate the profound impact this technology could have on AI development. By 2019, Cerebras Systems had raised over $200 million in venture funding, an endorsement of the startup's promise and potential.

Although they initially faced skepticism about their ability to deliver on their ambitious promises, they proved the critics wrong. The first WSE chips were shipped in 2019 to select partners and research institutions, where they outperformed existing hardware by significant margins. By 2020, they were made widely available for commercial use.

But it wasn't just about creating a powerful chip. The team at Cerebras had to consider the ethical ramifications of their work. The WSE, with its immense computing power, could be used for both beneficial and harmful AI applications. To address these concerns, the company instituted stringent guidelines and vetting processes for potential customers, making sure their technology would be used responsibly.

Cerebras Systems continued to defy the norms of the tech industry. The company was valued at over $2.4 billion, but more than the numbers, it changed the landscape of AI computation. It proved that with the right combination of innovation, execution, and ethical consideration, even a startup could change the game, making previously unimaginable levels of AI computation not just possible, but accessible.

This story showcases how addressing a specific, critical need in the AI ecosystem can pave the way for unparalleled success. While AI is often associated with data and algorithms, Cerebras Systems reminds us that innovative hardware can be just as transformative.

The stories of these successful AI startups serve as both inspiration and roadmap. They illuminate the vast landscape of opportunities, from specialized hardware to intuitive software solutions, each venture tapping into a unique facet of AI's transformative power. These startups have not only survived but thrived in an industry characterized by relentless innovation and fierce competition. They teach us that in the realm of AI, the key to success often lies in identifying a gap, challenging the status quo, and relentlessly driving toward a solution—even when faced with skepticism or seemingly insurmountable obstacles. As we move ahead, let's delve into how you can take the first steps in your own AI journey, converting your innovative ideas into a full-fledged startup.

Creating Your AI Startup: The Step-By-Step Playbook

So, you're inspired and brimming with ideas—but how do you start your own AI venture? Stay tuned as we break down the journey from ideation to fruition, demystifying the process of turning your innovative concepts into a thriving business.

In the age of AI, the business terrain is wide open for those daring enough to venture into it. The question is: How can you translate a groundbreaking idea into a viable, successful business? Let's dive into a step-by-step playbook that draws from industry best practices, expert opinions, and reports from leading research organizations like Gartner, McKinsey, and Harvard Business Review. This isn't theory; this is a real-world guide designed to give you actionable steps to launch your own AI startup.

Validating Your AI Idea

Picture this: You're standing at the edge of a cliff, parachute strapped to your back, exhilarated and scared in equal measure. Taking a leap of faith by starting an AI startup feels a lot like that cliffside moment. However, unlike skydiving, there's no instructor to tell you when to jump. That decision is yours and yours alone. Validation is your equivalent of checking your parachute; it ensures you're not plummeting to your doom.

The Importance of Validation

The tech graveyard is full of startups that had amazing products but solved problems nobody cared about. Before you take the plunge, you need to know if there's a pool at the bottom or just hard, unforgiving ground. Validation helps you assess the market need for your AI solution.

The World Is Your Laboratory

You don't need a fancy lab or huge funding to validate your idea; you need to get out there and talk to people. Use social media surveys, online forums, or even one-on-one interviews to gather feedback. It's the Lean Startup methodology's idea of "getting out of the building," but adapted for the AI space.

A Lesson from Dropbox

Remember the early days of Dropbox? Instead of building a full-fledged product, founder Drew Houston made a simple video showing how Dropbox would work. The video went viral, and suddenly they had proof that people needed their solution.

The AI Angle

Now, when it comes to AI, validation takes on a new layer of complexity. You're not just validating a solution; you're also validating a technology. And that can be a bit like trying to build the plane while you're flying it. The field of AI is ever-changing; what's groundbreaking today might be old news tomorrow.

The point is, when validating an AI-based idea, you should not only look at the problem your AI is solving but also if your AI technology is sustainable, scalable, and, most importantly, if it can provide a solution more effectively than existing technologies.

The Hard Questions

Validation often means asking yourself tough questions. Is your AI-based solution really ten times better than the existing solutions? Is the market ready for it? What legislative and ethical issues might you run into? These aren't questions to brush aside; they form the bedrock of your future enterprise.

As you mull over these questions, don't just look for confirmation. Search for contradictory evidence too. If the data contradicts your hypothesis, that's not failure; that's learning. It's far better to discover a fundamental flaw in your idea now than after you've poured months or years of your life into it.

When you think you've got enough data, sit down and analyze it. Use tools like SWOT analysis, or employ frameworks like the Business Model Canvas to structure your findings. If the signs point towards a genuine market need for your solution, that's your green light to proceed to the next stage: Developing a Minimum Viable Product.

Now, building a MVP is more than just creating a stripped-down version of your final product. It's about delivering enough value to your early customers that they're willing to take a chance on a new, unproven solution. That's your first real test in the market, and how you handle it will set the tone for your startup's future.

So, get ready to move from idea to action. Strap in; the ride ahead promises to be an exhilarating one!

Developing a Minimum Viable Product (MVP)

Imagine you're an artist, brush in hand, staring at a blank canvas. The endless white space is both intimidating and exhilarating. Developing a Minimum Viable Product (MVP) feels a lot like that moment before the first stroke of paint hits the canvas. But instead of brush and pigment, your tools are algorithms and data sets, and your masterpiece is an AI solution waiting to be brought to life.

What's in a MVP?

At its core, a Minimum Viable Product is about minimalism, but not the kind where you sacrifice functionality for aesthetics. It's about creating a product with the least features necessary to satisfy early adopters. Your MVP should offer a solution to the problem you've validated in the market, nothing more, nothing less. It's tempting to add all the bells and whistles right from the get-go, but remember: Simple is smart.

Choose Your Battles

When you're short on resources, it's crucial to know where to channel your energy. Is your AI product a predictive analytics tool for retailers? Focus on getting the prediction algorithm right, and don't worry too much about the user interface yet. Each feature you decide to include should be directly tied to the core function of your product.

Spotify's Learning Curve

Let's talk about Spotify, which although not an AI startup, exemplifies MVP perfectly. When it first launched, Spotify didn't have playlists, a radio feature, or even a mobile app. It was a desktop application that allowed users to search for a song and play it. That's it. But it solved a problem — illegal downloads — and provided a quicker, easier, and legal way to listen to music. They added other features only after validating the initial concept.

Data, Data, Data

In the AI landscape, data is as valuable as gold. Start collecting it from Day One. This will not only help in fine-tuning your algorithms but also prove invaluable when you're pitching to investors. Data provides credibility; it's concrete evidence that your product works and is needed in the market.

Data Privacy and Compliance

Since we're talking about data, it's crucial to mention data privacy laws like GDPR in the European Union or CCPA in California. It's not the most exciting topic, but ignoring it could lead to the death of your startup. Make sure your MVP complies with all relevant data protection regulations.

Iterate and Pivot

The beauty of an MVP lies in its flexibility. Once your product is in the hands of early adopters, listen to their feedback like it's gospel. These initial users are your most valuable source of information. They'll point out bugs you didn't know existed, suggest features you hadn't thought of, and their behavior will show you which aspects of your product are genuinely useful.

Setting Milestones

While developing your MVP, it's crucial to set both short-term and long-term milestones. These can act as guideposts, helping you stay on track and focused. More importantly, milestones can be incredibly motivating for your team, giving everyone a sense of accomplishment and direction.

Cash Flows and Bootstrapping

You might not be making money off your MVP immediately, but it can help in other ways. A well-designed MVP can be an excellent tool for fundraising. It demonstrates to potential investors that you have more than just an idea, you have something tangible and potentially lucrative.

Now, having navigated the treacherous waters of MVP development, what's next? Ah, you'll need the fuel to propel your startup into the stratosphere. And by fuel, I mean capital. The journey towards securing that capital promises to be an adventure of its own, replete with dragons to slay and mazes to navigate. Are you ready? Because the chapter on fundraising strategies is where we equip you with your sword and shield.

This stage sets the stage for a closer look at the financial backbone of your enterprise. While your idea and MVP are crucial, without the right financial strategies, even the most brilliant innovations can fizzle out.

Fundraising Strategies

In a world where ideas are the new currency, capital is the marketplace where they're bought and sold. Think of fundraising not as a chore, but as an opportunity to market your product, your team, and your vision to those who have the means to elevate it from a prototype to a world-changing technology.

Deciphering the ABCs of VC

Venture Capitalists (VCs) are often the knights in shining armor for startups, but be aware: their money comes with strings attached. VCs usually look for startups with high growth potential and exit strategies, and they'll often want equity and a board seat in return for their investment. When approaching VCs, arm yourself with a pitch deck that could convince even the most hardened skeptic. Include your unique value proposition, your go-to-market strategy, and financial projections. The more homework you've done, the better.

Angels and Seed Funds

Angels are high-net-worth individuals who invest smaller amounts than VCs, often in exchange for equity or convertible debt. Seed funds operate similarly, but might also provide mentorship, office space, and other perks. Platforms like AngelList have democratized this form of fundraising, connecting startups with hundreds of potential investors through a single pitch. It's like online dating, but for business.

Bootstrapping and Grants

Let's say you're not keen on relinquishing equity or control over your startup. In that case, bootstrapping by funding the business through personal savings or revenues could be an option. Alternatively, look for grants, especially those designed for technological innovation. Many governments offer financial incentives for research and development activities. It might not be as glamorous as a million-dollar investment round, but it's money you won't have to repay or give up equity for.

Due Diligence is a Two-way Street

As much as investors will scrutinize your startup, you should be analyzing them too. Look for investors who bring more than just capital to the table, such as industry connections, expertise, or resources that could facilitate growth.

The Emotional Quotient

Fundraising is an emotionally draining process. It's not for the faint-hearted. Rejection is part of the game, but each 'no' takes you one step closer to that exhilarating 'yes'. Use the feedback from unsuccessful pitches to refine your proposal and improve your chances in the future. Emotional resilience isn't just a valuable trait here; it's a survival tool.

As we close the chapter on fundraising strategies, we find

ourselves peering into the social fabric of your startup: the team. Because even a well-funded venture can crumble if the human element isn't right. The perfect alchemy of skills, personalities, and leadership can turn a promising startup into a tech unicorn. So, let's explore how you can orchestrate this harmony and create a team that becomes the lifeblood of your AI startup's success. Shall we?

Team Building

If your startup were a symphony, your team would be the orchestra. It's one thing to have a sheet of music; it's another thing entirely to have a group of individuals who can bring that composition to life.

Identifying Key Roles

Building a startup team is not about filling seats; it's about finding the right players for each position. In the world of AI startups, this often means having a mix of roles like data scientists, machine learning engineers, product managers, and UX/UI designers. Each role is critical and complements the others, forming a balanced, cohesive unit.

Culture, Culture, Culture

Work culture isn't about ping-pong tables and free snacks; it's about creating an environment where people can thrive, both personally and professionally. Companies like Google and Netflix aren't famous just for their products; they're renowned for their work culture. It's a factor that could make or break your startup, affecting everything from talent retention to overall productivity.

The Hiring Process

The classic dilemma for startups is whether to hire for skill or potential. There's no one-size-fits-all answer, but one principle stands: hire people who are smarter than you. You want a team that challenges you, pushes your boundaries, and makes you revisit your assumptions. And yes, this might make you uncomfortable, but that discomfort is a sign of growth, both for you and your startup.

Now that you've navigated the intricate web of team dynamics, what lies ahead is arguably the most exhilarating and challenging phase of your startup journey: scaling. It's where dreams are realized or shattered, where leaders are made or broken. Are you ready to unravel the mysteries of scaling your AI startup? Because that's where we're headed next. Hold on tight; it promises to be a thrilling ride.

Scaling Strategies

Scaling is akin to nurturing a sapling. Initially, it's about ensuring the roots are firm and the plant gets the essentials it needs. As it grows, the dynamics change; it requires more space, deeper roots, and consistent care to flourish into a sturdy tree. In a startup's journey, scaling is that phase where a founder's vision transforms into a tangible reality, expanding beyond its initial boundaries. Here's how to approach this critical stage with tact and acumen.

1. Understand the Difference Between Growth and Scaling

Growth and **scaling** are often used interchangeably but are distinctly different. Growth often signifies a linear progression—more hires, more customers, more output. It might mean that your costs and resources grow at the same rate as your revenue. Scaling, on the other hand, is about increasing revenue without a substantial increase in resources. It's about efficiency and increasing profit margins.

For instance, WhatsApp, at the time of its acquisition by Facebook, had 600 million users but only 50 employees. That's scaling in its true essence: serving a mammoth user base without a proportionate increase in team size.

2. Optimize Before You Expand

Before diving headfirst into expansion, ensure that your core processes are streamlined. Often, inefficiencies at a small scale become glaring problems when magnified. Are your current customers satisfied? Is your product free from major glitches? Iron out the creases in your foundation before constructing the next level.

Consider companies like Zappos, which built an impeccable customer service model before even thinking of massive expansion. Their focus on core values and providing unparalleled service made their subsequent scaling smooth and efficient.

3. Strategic Hiring for Scaling

While in the initial stages, you might have hired jacks-of-all-trades, scaling requires more specialized roles. It's also the stage where middle management becomes crucial. These individuals bridge the gap between the vision of top-tier leadership and the ground realities of execution teams.

Think about how Netflix pivoted from a DVD rental service to a streaming giant. This transition required hiring experts in streaming technology, content creation, and global marketing.

4. Diversify Revenue Streams

Relying on a single source of revenue can be perilous. Exploring various monetization models and diversifying revenue streams can cushion against market volatilities. Look at Apple; what started as a computer company now earns significantly from its App Store, services, and wearables.

5. Technology is Your Ally

Invest in technology that makes scaling easier. Automate repetitive tasks, use data analytics to understand customer behavior, and embrace AI and machine learning to refine your offerings. Dropbox, for instance, used clever referral programs with tech integration to grow its user base exponentially without proportionate marketing spends.

6. Maintain Culture Amidst Rapid Change

Scaling can sometimes make a company lose its essence. As teams grow and dynamics shift, it's paramount to ensure that the core values and culture remain intact. No matter how large Google grows, its core principle of 'Don't be evil' remains a guiding force.

In conclusion, scaling isn't merely about getting bigger; it's about getting better, smarter, and more efficient. As you transition from a startup to a more established entity, remember that each phase has its own challenges and rewards. Embrace the journey, learn from the missteps, and always aim for sustainable, thoughtful growth. As you move forward, equipped with these strategies and insights, you're well on your way to etching your startup's name in the annals of success.

Action Steps for Creating Your AI Startup

In this chapter, we've navigated the complex yet exciting waters of launching and scaling an AI startup. We discussed critical stages, from initial idea validation to early-stage planning, fundraising strategies, team building, and finally, scaling your venture. By applying the knowledge encapsulated in this chapter, entrepreneurs can arm themselves with a comprehensive toolkit to succeed in the AI landscape.

Action Steps:

1. **Idea Validation**:

   - Conduct a SWOT (Strengths, Weaknesses, Opportunities, Threats) analysis.

   - Create a minimum viable product (MVP) to test your idea in the real world.

2. **Market Research**:

   - Identify target customer personas.

   - Analyze market size and potential for scale.

3. **Legal Foundation**:

   - Register the company and get the legal basics in place.

   - Obtain all necessary patents, copyrights, and trademarks.

4. **Business Plan**:

   - Outline your mission, vision, short-term and

long-term goals.

- Create financial projections for at least 5 years.

5. **Fundraising**:

   - Prepare a solid pitch deck.

   - Reach out to angel investors, VCs, or consider bootstrapping.

6. **Team Building**:

   - Hire strategically, focusing on immediate needs and future scalability.

   - Develop an organizational structure that facilitates easy communication and task delegation.

7. **Product Development**:

   - Build the MVP if you haven't already.

   - Use agile methodologies for iterative development and improvement.

8. **Go-to-Market Strategy**:

   - Select the appropriate market channels.

   - Develop an initial customer acquisition strategy.

9. **Scaling**:

   - Optimize your business model for scalability.

   - Diversify revenue streams and focus on customer retention.

10. **Continuous Learning and Adaptation**:

- Keep an eye on market trends and emerging technologies.

- Iterate and adapt as needed.

Checklist:

- ⬜ Idea is validated through SWOT and MVP.

- ⬜ Market research is complete.

- ⬜ Legal formalities are taken care of.

- ⬜ Business plan is prepared and reviewed.

- ⬜ Fundraising avenues are explored and secured.

- ⬜ Core team members are onboard.

- ⬜ MVP or full product is developed.

- ⬜ Go-to-market strategy is implemented.

- ⬜ Business is ready for scaling.

- ⬜ Continuous improvement mechanisms are in place.

Roadmap:

1. **Quarter 1**: Idea validation and market research.

2. **Quarter 2**: Legal setup and initial team building.

3. **Quarter 3**: Business planning and beginning of fundraising.

4. **Quarter 4**: Complete fundraising and finalize MVP.

5. **Year 1, Q1-Q2**: Launch MVP, go-to-market strategy implementation.

6. **Year 1, Q3-Q4**: Initial scaling efforts.

7. **Year 2 onwards**: More significant scaling, diversification, and growth.

While the steps and strategies outlined in this chapter equip you with a robust toolkit for AI entrepreneurship, the transformative power of artificial intelligence isn't reserved for startups alone. Its potential is something that everyone—be it an individual or a large corporation—can tap into for innovation and improvement. As we transition into the next part of this book, we'll explore how you, as an individual, can leverage AI in your day-to-day life to become an Everyday Innovator. Stay tuned; the world of AI has something for everyone.

Part IV: The Everyday Innovator: AI for the Individual

Automate Your Skills: How AI Can Amplify Your Talents

Ever wondered how you could get a leg up in your career or hobby by using the same technology that's revolutionizing industries? Artificial intelligence is no longer the sole domain of giant tech companies and ambitious startups. It's something that can work for you, amplify your talents, and give you a competitive edge in ways you've never imagined.

Writing Enhanced by AI

When we think of writing, the image that often comes to mind is a solitary figure, hunched over a typewriter or a laptop, lost in thought. But what if this individual had a secret weapon? A tool that could review their work, suggest improvements, and even assist in generating content?

Imagine, for instance, the life of Sarah, a freelance writer who used to spend hours editing her work. As deadlines loomed, the stress would increase, leaving her anxious and overwhelmed. Sarah then discovered AI-based writing assistants. It was as if a weight had been lifted. These tools scanned her articles, pointed out grammatical errors, and suggested more effective ways to phrase her ideas. Over time, not only did the quality of her writing improve, but she also started getting more freelance gigs.

But it wasn't just about correcting grammar. Advanced AI algorithms can analyze text for tone, coherence, and even emotional impact. Sarah also began to use AI tools that could suggest topics based on trending themes and generate outlines for her articles.

When it comes to leveraging AI in writing, the options are almost limitless. Imagine an AI tool that can help draft emails or reports, allowing you to focus on the conceptual and creative aspects of your job. Picture a novelist using an AI assistant to plot story arcs, or a marketer using machine learning algorithms to write copy that resonates perfectly with the target audience.

One could argue that the rise of such tools could make human writers obsolete, but the key is to see these tools as collaborators, not competitors. AI can handle the manual, repetitive aspects of writing, but it lacks the emotional intelligence and the nuanced understanding of human experiences that only a human writer can bring to the table.

From Sarah's story, we can learn that using AI tools for writing isn't about outsourcing your job to a machine; it's about letting the machine handle the drudgery so you can focus on the creative and intellectual aspects of writing. With the burden of monotonous tasks lifted, imagine the masterpieces you could create, the stories you could tell, and the impact you could have.

This is more than a technological innovation; it's a new way of thinking about skills and productivity. In the next section, we'll explore how AI can similarly revolutionize the world of graphic design, transforming how visuals are created and understood. So, if you thought AI in writing was transformative, buckle up because you're in for an equally inspiring ride in the realm of design.

AI in Graphic Design

The world of graphic design has undergone a seismic shift thanks to AI technology. Gone are the days when you needed an arsenal of complicated software and an intricate knowledge of design principles. Today, AI can perform tasks ranging from automating mundane activities like cropping and resizing to providing design suggestions that are empirically likely to attract more attention.

Consider Emily, a graphic designer whose forte is in creating stunning visual content for digital marketing campaigns. Despite her talent, she often found herself bogged down with repetitive tasks. She would spend hours tweaking minor details, leaving her little time to focus on the conceptual and innovative aspects of her work. That was until she discovered AI-powered design tools that automated many of these time-consuming activities.

These intelligent programs could automatically select complementary color schemes based on a company's brand guidelines, generate design templates, and even create whole sets of marketing collateral with a few clicks. These tools were learning from each design Emily made, suggesting more personalized and effective design elements as time went on.

But automation was just one part of the story. AI also brought predictive analytics into Emily's workflow. Through machine learning, her AI tool could predict consumer responses to different visual elements, thereby creating more effective designs. For instance, the software could analyze thousands of successful marketing campaigns to determine which types of images, color schemes, or fonts were most likely to engage a specific demographic. Emily could then use these insights to create more impactful designs from the get-go.

What's striking is that Emily started receiving accolades for her creative breakthroughs. Not only was her work more effective, but she also found she had more time to focus on expanding her skill set, trying new techniques, and truly pushing the boundaries of what she could create. She had the freedom to experiment, and her work started to receive attention from industry leaders and influencers.

However, like any tool, AI in graphic design also has its limitations. While it can provide suggestions and automate tasks, it lacks the nuance and intuition that a human designer brings to the table. It can analyze past data but can't envision the future trends that a creative mind might perceive. But rather than replacing human creativity, AI serves to augment it. The machine takes care of the manual labor, leaving the human mind free to do what it does best: create, innovate, and inspire.

As we delve further into how AI can be harnessed by individuals, it's crucial to remember that these tools are meant to be extensions of our own abilities. As we've seen in both writing and design, AI can remove barriers, granting us more space to elevate our creativity to new heights. However, as we amplify our skills with AI, it's also imperative to be mindful of the ethical dimensions, a topic we'll examine closely later in this chapter.

Our next part will delve into the fascinating interplay between music and artificial intelligence, where beats, chords, and melodies are algorithmically woven into a new kind of symphony. The future of individual skill enhancement has never looked brighter.

AI in Music Composition

We've been exploring a truly transformative journey, witnessing firsthand how artificial intelligence enables us to become virtuosos in our own right—regardless of the arena, be it writing or graphic design. Now, let's explore the magical interplay between music and AI.

Imagine you're Joshua, a musician dabbling in various genres but particularly fascinated by electronic music. Your ambition to create a chart-topping album is often dampened by the limitations of your small home studio and, more so, by the complexity of learning multiple music software suites. Not to mention, producing music involves an intricate blend of creativity and technical knowledge, from understanding scales and chords to mastering and mixing.

Enter AI-powered music composition tools. For Joshua, this was nothing short of a musical renaissance. These AI tools analyze thousands—sometimes millions—of songs to understand the structures, rhythms, and harmonies that resonate with listeners. Using this knowledge, they can suggest chord progressions, generate instrumental solos, or even create an entire composition from scratch.

Joshua was enamored with how the AI tool helped him overcome creative blocks. Stuck on a melody? The tool could offer a range of options to complement the existing musical elements. Need to add a bridge? A few clicks would generate several possibilities, complete with orchestration and even harmonic complexity that would cater to his specified genre.

But the AI didn't just act as a co-composer; it also became Joshua's mentor. While working, he started understanding why certain chord progressions worked and why specific notes resonated better. The software also provided real-time analytics about how different elements of his compositions could impact listener engagement, tapping into behavioral psychology aspects of music. His music became not just a series of notes but an experiment in resonating with human emotion.

However, the AI tool wasn't an end-all solution. It couldn't replicate the raw emotion that Joshua could pour into a melody or the unique musical idiosyncrasies that defined his style. Moreover, Joshua was cautious about overly depending on AI. Could a machine-generated composition ever truly be called 'his work'? This led him to strike a balance, using AI for inspiration and technical guidance but ensuring the emotional core of his music remained human.

As he navigated his AI-augmented creative journey, Joshua started producing tracks that were both critically acclaimed and commercially successful. AI didn't take away from his music; it elevated it to a level he had never imagined possible.

Joshua's story serves as a compelling testament to the limitless possibilities when human creativity is complemented by AI's brute analytical power. Whether you're an author, a designer, or a musician, AI doesn't take away your uniqueness; it amplifies it. But as we enjoy this amplified creativity, we should also think about the ethical aspects—such as data privacy and the potential for AI to perpetuate existing biases.

Data Science for Non-Data Scientists

When we think about data science, our minds often go straight to the geeks and the nerds of the world, sitting in a dimly lit room surrounded by multiple screens displaying codes and numbers. But what if I told you that data science is not just for the statistically inclined or the programming savvy? It's a field that can help you, yes you, make more informed decisions, understand your habits, predict outcomes, and basically give you superpowers—well, intellectual ones at least.

The revolution started a few years back, with the inception of user-friendly tools that started to democratize the data science field. Today, we have various platforms, free and subscription-based, that can teach you data science in a way that feels more like a fun hobby than work. But, let's cut to the chase: Why should you care?

Imagine being able to predict consumer behavior for your small online business, or getting insights into the health of your plants based on soil quality, or even being able to predict your city's weather more accurately than the local meteorologist. While these examples seem broad, they are real-world applications that have been made easy enough for a layperson to execute.

Here's the thing: AI is driving this democratization. Tools are being developed that allow you to drag and drop variables into a user-friendly interface, and lo and behold, you get a prediction or a pattern. That's the power of machine learning algorithms today. They can be complex to set up, but thanks to these user-friendly tools, you don't have to.

Of course, data science still involves a good amount of, well, science. You need data to analyze, and while platforms today come with tons of pre-loaded data sets, your unique requirements may necessitate a little data gathering. That's where AI can also help. There are AI algorithms that can scour the web to collect data for you, based on parameters you define. All this information can be compiled and prepared for analysis, sometimes with little to no manual intervention. This isn't just convenience; this is revolutionizing how we do research, how we prepare reports, and how we look at data.

However, it's essential to understand the ethical

considerations. Data privacy is a significant concern, and any AI tool that gathers data needs to comply with data protection laws like GDPR in Europe or CCPA in California. These tools are designed to respect privacy, but the onus is also on you to be vigilant and ensure you're not crossing any boundaries.

By now, you should be feeling at least a little bit excited. There's a whole world of data science out there just waiting for you to dive in. Whether you're a writer, a marketer, a gardener, or a city planner, the applications are endless. You just need to take that first step. So what's holding you back?

Data Science for Non-Data Scientists

When we think about data science, our minds often go straight to the geeks and the nerds of the world, sitting in a dimly lit room surrounded by multiple screens displaying codes and numbers. But what if I told you that data science is not just for the statistically inclined or the programming savvy? It's a field that can help you, yes you, make more informed decisions, understand your habits, predict outcomes, and basically give you superpowers—well, intellectual ones at least.

The revolution started a few years back, with the inception of user-friendly tools that started to democratize the data science field. Today, we have various platforms, free and subscription-based, that can teach you data science in a way that feels more like a fun hobby than work. But, let's cut to the chase: Why should you care?

Imagine being able to predict consumer behavior for your small online business, or getting insights into the health of your plants based on soil quality, or even being able to predict your city's weather more accurately than the local meteorologist. While these examples seem broad, they are real-world applications that have been made easy enough for a layperson to execute.

Here's the thing: AI is driving this democratization. Tools are being developed that allow you to drag and drop variables into a user-friendly interface, and lo and behold, you get a prediction or a pattern. That's the power of machine learning algorithms today. They can be complex to set up, but thanks to these user-friendly tools, you don't have to.

Of course, data science still involves a good amount of, well, science. You need data to analyze, and while platforms today come with tons of pre-loaded data sets, your unique requirements may necessitate a little data gathering. That's where AI can also help. There are AI algorithms that can scour the web to collect data for you, based on parameters you define. All this information can be compiled and prepared for analysis, sometimes with little to no manual intervention. This isn't just convenience; this is revolutionizing how we do research, how we prepare reports, and how we look at data.

However, it's essential to understand the ethical considerations. Data privacy is a significant concern, and any AI tool that gathers data needs to comply with data protection laws like GDPR in Europe or CCPA in California. These tools are designed to respect privacy, but the onus is also on you to be vigilant and ensure you're not crossing any boundaries.

By now, you should be feeling at least a little bit excited. There's a whole world of data science out there just waiting for you to dive in. Whether you're a writer, a marketer, a gardener, or a city planner, the applications are endless. You just need to take that first step. So what's holding you back?

AI in Home DIY Projects

When it comes to do-it-yourself (DIY) projects, most people's minds probably drift toward building a bookshelf or maybe installing a new kitchen sink. But the world of DIY has gone digital, and AI is right at the center of it. Yes, you can use AI in your home DIY projects, and you don't have to be a computer scientist or a machine learning expert to do it.

Let's start with the most obvious application: home automation. While commercially available smart home systems can be expensive and sometimes limiting, you can actually create a budget-friendly, AI-powered smart home system yourself. It might sound like the plot of a sci-fi movie, but we're already there. You can control your lights, your thermostat, and even your coffee maker, all thanks to AI and a little creativity.

How about gardening? Did you know that you could build an AI-based irrigation system that waters your plants based on soil moisture levels? Or let's take it up a notch: you could even set up a plant recognition system in your garden. Picture this, a camera-based system that recognizes different types of plants and weeds. No more pulling up your prized petunias instead of those pesky weeds. All you need is a simple Raspberry Pi computer, a camera, and a little AI magic, and your garden could be the talk of the town.

AI can also help with more complex DIY projects. Have you ever dreamed of building your own drone? You can do that now. With open-source AI algorithms available for object detection, path planning, and stabilization, your drone could not only fly but also interact with its environment in sophisticated ways. Imagine a drone that could automatically detect and follow specific wildlife for your photography hobby or one that could map out a hiking trail for you.

But it's not just about projects that are "cool"; they can be practical and potentially life-changing too. Home security is a huge concern for many, and AI can offer solutions that are both cost-effective and cutting-edge. An AI-based facial recognition system can be integrated into your home security system, instantly alerting you if someone unrecognized is on your property. This doesn't require an army of developers or a mountain of cash. The code for such projects is often freely available, and the hardware can be surprisingly affordable.

Speaking of code, you don't need to be a programming whiz to make this happen. Today, AI platforms offer what is known as 'low-code' or 'no-code' options, allowing individuals with minimal coding experience to create AI algorithms for specific tasks. You might have to learn some basics, but you certainly won't need a degree in computer science.

This brings us back to the question of ethics, especially when dealing with things like facial recognition in home security. The technology is powerful, but it also comes with significant ethical considerations. Consent and data security are crucial when implementing such systems. Fortunately, the AI community is vocal about these issues, and guidelines exist to help DIYers stay on the right path.

AI for home DIY projects is like an undiscovered treasure trove. Every day, people around the world are coming up with new, amazing ways to incorporate AI into their home projects. They aren't experts or engineers, just enthusiastic individuals ready to dive into the future, one project at a time. So why not join them? After all, the future is not just for the experts; it's for everyone.

Real-World Examples: People Who've Successfully Used AI to Amplify Their Skills

Every technological revolution has its set of pioneers, and AI is no different. However, unlike past revolutions, the rise of AI has been somewhat unique in its accessibility. One no longer needs to be part of a gigantic corporate conglomerate or a government organization to make strides in technology. In fact, the democratization of AI has allowed everyday individuals to achieve monumental tasks, things that would have required a team of experts and millions of dollars just a few years ago.

Take the case of Sarah, a high-school teacher passionate about ecology and environment conservation. She was increasingly worried about the declining population of a particular bird species in her local area. Using some cheap sensors, a low-cost computer like a Raspberry Pi, and a freely available AI algorithm, she set up a system that could identify and count the species' appearances in multiple locations. The data was then compiled and analyzed to get an accurate estimation of the population and its movement patterns. Sarah's efforts caught the attention of local conservation bodies and provided valuable data that could be used for conservation efforts. She had no prior knowledge of AI or programming but managed to change the future for an entire species in her local area.

Or consider Tim, a retired civil engineer who took to farming. Agriculture is an area where AI has shown significant promise, but most examples are large-scale applications designed for industrial farming. Tim, however, used AI to optimize the watering schedule for his small but diverse vegetable farm. Using soil moisture sensors and local weather data, the AI model he implemented optimized the watering schedule to the point where he reduced water consumption by 25% without affecting the yield. In fact, the yield increased by 10% compared to the previous non-AI-optimized methods.

What about Jane, a freelance writer who was battling tight deadlines and a highly competitive market? By using AI tools that helped her in quick research, generating outlines, and even editing her work, she managed to increase her productivity by leaps and bounds. These weren't advanced AI models but simple browser-based tools that anyone can use. The increase in her efficiency not only allowed her to take on more work but also significantly improved the quality of her writing.

And then there's Raj, an amateur musician who used AI to compose music for his YouTube channel. Lacking formal training in music theory, Raj turned to AI algorithms that could create background scores based on the mood and tempo he wanted. As of last count, he had over 50,000 subscribers and was making a decent side income, all thanks to the AI model that turned his musical thoughts into reality.

Stories like these are not isolated incidents; they're signs of a sweeping change where AI becomes a lever for amplifying human potential. These individuals didn't start as experts in AI; they started as experts in caring about something. And that is all you really need. With the available resources, online communities, and technologies, anyone willing to invest some time can harness the power of AI to make substantial changes in their lives and the lives of others.

These stories prove that the power of AI is not just reserved for corporations, research institutions, or governments. It's also accessible to individuals who can use it as a tool to improve, optimize, and even revolutionize their pursuits. It underscores the fact that AI isn't the future; it's the present, and it's entirely within your grasp.

Your AI Skillset: A Blueprint to Get Started

When we read or hear about AI, it's easy to get overwhelmed by the technical jargon and complex algorithms that seem almost incomprehensible. But here's the good news: You don't have to be a programming whiz or a mathematical genius to benefit from AI. The key is to approach AI not as a monolithic subject but as a collection of tools that can be combined in creative ways to solve specific problems. It's a bit like playing with LEGO; you pick and choose the pieces that fit your project.

Let's begin by understanding that AI is not just one thing; it's a field that covers everything from machine learning algorithms to natural language processing and robotics. To harness AI effectively, you don't need to know everything; you need to know what's relevant to your objectives.

So, how does one begin this journey? First, you must define what you want to achieve. Are you looking to automate a repetitive task, gain insights from data, or create something entirely new? Once you've clearly defined your objectives, the next step is to acquire the right tools for the job. The good thing is that many of these tools are available for free or at a minimal cost. For instance, Python, one of the most popular programming languages for AI, has a plethora of free resources and libraries like TensorFlow and PyTorch that can help you set the foundation for your AI project.

But what if coding isn't your forte? That's not a problem either. We are in an age where user-friendly AI platforms have started to emerge. These platforms offer pre-built algorithms and models that can be customized for your specific needs. No coding needed. Tools like Google's AutoML or IBM's Watson Studio provide a graphical interface where you can train, evaluate, and deploy AI models by merely dragging and dropping.

For those who are not entirely averse to coding but don't have advanced skills, there's a middle path. Many AI tasks can be accomplished using simple scripts. There are countless tutorials online that guide you through these processes, often with ready-to-use code snippets that you can directly implement into your projects. It's a bit like cooking; you don't have to be a chef to follow a recipe.

Learning by doing is the most effective way to understand the capabilities and limitations of AI. Start with a small, manageable project and gradually move to more complex tasks as you get comfortable. Join online forums or local meetups to collaborate with like-minded individuals. Learning from others' experiences, both successes and failures, can be invaluable in accelerating your learning curve.

So, where can you find these resources? Open-source platforms like GitHub offer a treasure trove of project examples and code snippets. Websites like Coursera and Udacity offer specialized AI courses, many of which are free or offer free trials. There are also tons of free e-books, blogs, and YouTube tutorials that can help you at every stage of your AI journey.

Remember, Rome wasn't built in a day. Mastery over AI is not an overnight achievement but a process that involves continuous learning and experimentation. However, it's a journey well worth taking, as the examples from our previous section clearly demonstrate.

Ethical Considerations: Navigating the Do's and Don'ts

As the saying goes, "With great power comes great responsibility." Nowhere is this truer than in the realm of AI. As you embark on your journey to harness the capabilities of artificial intelligence, there are ethical considerations that should guide your actions at every step of the way. And these are not just superficial guidelines; they are the bedrock on which the future of AI is being built.

Privacy concerns are at the forefront of AI ethics. If your project involves collecting data, especially personal or sensitive information, you need to be extra cautious. The data should be anonymized, encrypted, and stored securely, adhering to the various privacy laws like GDPR in Europe or CCPA in California. More importantly, the data should only be used for the purpose for which it was collected. Misuse or unauthorized access could lead to severe penalties, both legal and reputational.

Inclusivity is another important ethical consideration. When building AI models, it's crucial to ensure that the data set used for training is diverse and represents the target population adequately. An AI model trained on a skewed dataset can result in biased or discriminatory outcomes. Such errors are not just bad for business but can also perpetuate social inequalities.

Transparency is a core tenet of ethical AI. If your AI model impacts people's lives in any way, it's essential to explain how decisions are made. Known as explainable AI, this field focuses on making the decision-making process of AI systems as transparent as possible. Whether you're using AI to determine loan eligibility or medical diagnosis, users have the right to know how these determinations are made.

Beyond these fundamentals, there's the question of fairness. AI systems should aim to treat all individuals and groups impartially. However, ensuring fairness is not always straightforward, as it often involves tackling complex social and cultural factors. Moreover, algorithms that appear fair can sometimes lead to unfair outcomes due to hidden biases in the data or the people who create these algorithms. Therefore, continuous monitoring and adjustment are necessary.

One might wonder, how can an individual make a meaningful impact in this landscape of ethical complexities? Well, it starts with awareness. Before initiating any project, take the time to understand the ethical implications involved. Consult experts, adhere to industry standards, and be willing to pivot your approach if it conflicts with ethical guidelines.

Many organizations are providing frameworks to assist in navigating the ethical dimensions of AI. For example, the Institute of Electrical and Electronics Engineers (IEEE) has published detailed guidelines on Ethically Aligned Design in AI. These documents offer practical advice on how to approach AI projects with ethical integrity.

Moreover, ethical AI is not just a matter of compliance; it's a competitive advantage. Consumers and clients are increasingly aware of the ethical implications of technology. By adhering to the highest ethical standards, you not only mitigate risks but also enhance your brand's reputation and trustworthiness.

So, how do we navigate this minefield of ethical dilemmas?

1. **Education and Awareness**: Both AI practitioners and the general public need to be educated about the ethical implications of AI. A well-informed populace can advocate for responsible AI use.

2. **Diverse and Inclusive Training Data**: Ensuring that training data is diverse and representative can mitigate the risk of biased AI models.

3. **Ethical Guidelines**: Organizations, both public and private, should have clear ethical guidelines for AI deployment. These guidelines should be regularly reviewed and updated.

4. **Transparency and Explainability**: Investing in research that makes AI models more transparent and understandable is crucial. OpenAI, among others, is working on this front.

5. **Regulations**: While over-regulation can stifle innovation, a complete lack of regulation is equally dangerous. Governments around the world are now considering and enacting AI-specific regulations to

ensure responsible development and use.

6. **Stakeholder Involvement**: Decisions about AI deployment shouldn't be left to tech experts alone. It requires collaboration between technologists, ethicists, sociologists, and the public at large.

The path to ethical AI is neither straightforward nor static. As AI technologies evolve, so too will the ethical challenges they pose. Yet, by proactively addressing these issues, we can ensure that the benefits of AI are realized while minimizing potential harm.

The Future of Individual Skill Enhancement Through AI

Artificial Intelligence has had a transformative effect on a multitude of sectors, from healthcare and finance to education and entertainment. However, what is increasingly capturing the public's imagination is how this technology can amplify individual skills, fundamentally altering the way we work, learn, and even interact with the world. As we stand on the brink of this brave new era, let's delve into the compelling future of individual skill enhancement through AI.

Let's imagine a day in the not-so-distant future. You wake up, and your AI personal assistant briefs you on your day, highlighting the skills you'll need for various tasks. For a crucial client meeting, it has already analyzed millions of successful negotiations and offers you tailored strategies. Your AI-driven language learning system recommends you brush up on your Mandarin, as one of the stakeholders is a native speaker. At the meeting, real-time language translation helps you and your Chinese counterpart communicate effortlessly.

Later, you're working on a graphic design project. Your AI assistant, trained on an enormous dataset of award-winning designs, suggests creative concepts that match the client's brand ethos. It also advises you on the color theory and even auto-generates a few design options, drastically reducing the time you'd otherwise spend on this task.

Even skills that we think of as inherently human could be enhanced. Take emotional intelligence as an example. Companies are already working on AI systems that can read human emotions by analyzing facial expressions, vocal tones, and body language. While it sounds like science fiction, these technologies could help people understand social cues better, enhancing their emotional intelligence in both personal and professional settings.

The integration of AI in skill enhancement is not a one-size-fits-all solution but will be increasingly customized. AI systems are expected to adapt to individual learning styles, paces, and preferences. Whether you are a visual learner, prefer hands-on experience, or learn best through reading, future AI systems will curate tailored learning paths, constantly adjusting to optimize your skill development.

Let's also talk about accessibility. Advanced skills that were once the exclusive domain of experts could become accessible to a broader audience. Imagine AI-powered legal research assistants making it easier for non-lawyers to understand complex legislation, or AI-driven medical diagnostic tools democratizing healthcare knowledge. The lowering of these 'skill barriers' could revolutionize how we think about expertise and specialization.

Of course, this future isn't without its challenges. Ethical considerations, as discussed in the previous section, loom large. Ensuring equitable access to these AI tools will be essential. There's a real risk of widening the skill gap between those who can afford these advanced AI systems and those who can't. Thus, policy interventions may be required to ensure that the future of skill enhancement is inclusive and available to all.

Furthermore, as AI systems play a larger role in our skill development, issues of dependency may arise. Balancing AI assistance with human intuition and creativity will be crucial. We must ensure that AI serves as a complementary tool that amplifies human skills rather than a crutch that leads to skill atrophy.

In summary, the future of individual skill enhancement through AI is tantalizingly within reach. We're looking at a revolution that won't just streamline tasks but can also make us better versions of ourselves, democratize access to advanced skills, and even redefine what it means to be skilled. However, this journey requires careful navigation, balancing technological possibilities with ethical imperatives. But one thing is clear: the symbiotic relationship between humans and AI is set to redefine the contours of individual capabilities in ways we are just beginning to understand.

Business Ideas for the Common Person: Turning AI into Gold

In this chapter, we'll explore a range of business ideas that are accessible to the "common person" but have the potential to yield extraordinary results. We'll cover sectors ripe for AI-driven innovation and introduce ideas that span the range of complexity and investment. Whether you're an individual with a knack for coding, a creative type interested in design, or someone in between, there's likely an AI-driven business opportunity that can work for you.

Leveraging AI for Content Creation.

Content creation is an arena that has been traditionally dominated by human ingenuity, creativity, and language skills. In the past, nothing could quite match the unique touch of human writers when it came to crafting a compelling story or an engaging article. But the age of AI has ushered in a host of changes that are rapidly altering this landscape. These changes aren't meant to replace humans but to work alongside them, enhancing their abilities and streamlining the creative process.

One of the most significant innovations in this area is the advent of Natural Language Processing (NLP) algorithms.

NLP is a subset of AI that focuses on the interaction between computers and human language. NLP algorithms can analyze text data, understand its context, and even generate human-like text based on the data it has been trained on. This innovation has far-reaching implications for content creation, from journalism to marketing, and beyond.

Journalistic Use Cases

The application of AI in journalism is becoming more widespread. News agencies are now using algorithms to churn out short news stories, particularly for topics that are straightforward and data-heavy, such as financial reports or sports scores. Even in more complex articles, AI can assist journalists by gathering and sorting through large volumes of data to find relevant information. In some cases, algorithms have been used to analyze social media trends and sentiments, providing journalists with valuable insights into public opinion on critical matters.

The technology isn't just limited to writing. AI tools are available that can automatically generate videos, infographics, and other multimedia content based on the text or data input they receive. These tools can be especially useful for media organizations that are working with limited resources.

Marketing Applications

In the field of marketing, the possibilities are equally enticing. Marketing firms are employing AI algorithms to generate promotional content, customer emails, and even social media posts. Imagine a small business owner who needs to manage multiple aspects of the business, including marketing. AI tools can automate the process of content creation, allowing the owner to focus on other core aspects of the business.

An AI-powered content generation tool can be set to understand the brand voice, target audience, and key messaging points. Once configured, it can auto-generate marketing copy that aligns with these parameters, saving both time and money. In an era where content is king, the ability to produce high-quality content at scale can provide a significant competitive edge.

Enhancing Creativity

AI doesn't mean the end of creativity; instead, it can act as a booster. AI algorithms can analyze vast amounts of data, including historical trends, consumer behavior, and competitive landscape, to provide suggestions that can help human creators. For instance, if you're a scriptwriter suffering from writer's block, AI tools can analyze successful scripts similar to your project and offer suggestions for plot points, dialogues, or character development.

Collaborative Content Creation

In an ever-more-connected world, the collaborative aspect of content creation can't be ignored. Gone are the days when a single author would pen down an entire novel in isolation. Today, content is often created by a team of writers, editors, designers, and marketers who work in harmony to produce the final product. Here, AI can serve as the invisible member of your team, sitting in on brainstorming sessions and offering valuable input.

For example, if you are a content team that frequently collaborates on documents, AI can help by flagging inconsistencies in the text, suggesting improvements for readability, and even offering SEO-friendly title suggestions. It can process the inputs of multiple team members in real-time, ensuring that the final product is cohesive and high-quality.

Scripting and Storyboarding

Another interesting application of AI in content creation is in the realm of scriptwriting and storyboarding for films and advertising campaigns. Complex algorithms can analyze the sequence of scenes, dialogues, and even camera angles used in popular movies or commercials and offer suggestions to enhance your script or storyboard. In fact, some Hollywood films are already employing AI to predict the success of a film based on its script, enabling them to make data-driven decisions on whether to go ahead with a project.

E-Books and Long-Form Content

Long-form content like e-books or whitepapers often requires an extensive amount of research, writing, and editing. AI tools can assist in all of these phases. Research can be expedited using algorithms that can sift through vast online repositories to find relevant information. AI can help outline the book, suggest headings, and even provide a rough draft that you can later refine.

Learning and Development

In the realm of education and training, AI is also proving to be a boon. Custom courses can be auto-generated based on the learning history and preferences of each individual, making the learning process much more efficient. For content creators in the educational sector, AI can suggest improvements or additions to course material based on real-time feedback and performance metrics from students.

User-Generated Content

Last but not least, let's talk about user-generated content (UGC). Platforms like YouTube, Instagram, and TikTok thrive on UGC, and here too, AI has a role to play. Algorithms can analyze trends and audience preferences, allowing creators to produce content that is more likely to be received well. More importantly, AI tools can also monitor for inappropriate content, ensuring that the platform remains a safe space for all users.

In summary, AI is not a threat but a collaborator in the journey of content creation. It's a tool that can make the process more efficient, effective, and even enjoyable. The key is to understand its capabilities and limitations, and to use it in a manner that complements human skills rather than replacing them.

AI-Driven Personal Finance

In the realm of personal finance, AI is not merely a futuristic concept but a transformative tool that's already reshaping how we manage our money. Consider an application that doesn't just categorize your expenses and track your budget. Imagine a tool that predicts future financial trends based on your behavior, advising you on investment opportunities, warning you of potential overspending, or even suggesting optimal moments to buy or sell assets.

The AI-driven finance apps of today are predictive, proactive, and personalized. They dig into historical data and ongoing behavior to forecast your financial future, generating insights that are incredibly personalized. It's like having a financial advisor in your pocket, available 24/7, except this one runs on algorithms and data analytics, and therefore, doesn't charge you an arm and a leg for its services.

So, what makes these AI-driven finance apps so revolutionary? Firstly, the algorithms can analyze vast amounts of data at lightning speeds, providing real-time insights that would take a human advisor days to calculate. Secondly, the predictive capabilities of these AI models get better with more data, meaning the longer you use the app, the more accurate and personalized its suggestions become.

Several fintech startups have already started leveraging this technology, offering predictive budgeting, automated investment services, and even AI-driven insurance quotes. Companies like Robinhood, Acorns, and others are changing the face of personal finance, and they're just the tip of the iceberg.

But it's not just about budgeting and investing. AI in personal finance extends to credit risk assessments, fraud detection, and even tax planning. Tax preparation apps, for instance, can sift through the labyrinthine tax code to find every deduction you're eligible for, potentially saving you a hefty sum each year.

Now, you might be thinking, "What's the catch?" Like every technology, AI-driven financial tools are not without their risks. There's the obvious concern about data privacy. After all, you're feeding these apps incredibly sensitive information. Therefore, always ensure that you're using trusted platforms that comply with data protection regulations.

Moreover, while AI can offer suggestions based on data, the decision to act on those suggestions is yours and should be made after thorough consideration. An algorithm won't understand the emotional or situational context; it can't know if you're planning a life change that might impact your finances.

That said, the benefits far outweigh the risks if used wisely. In a world that's becoming increasingly complex, having an AI-driven financial advisor can simplify your life, freeing up more time for you to do the things you love while ensuring that your future is secure.

The bottom line? AI-driven personal finance tools are no longer an optional luxury but a necessary asset for savvy financial planning.

Automated Design Services

As we've already seen, AI is democratizing skills and

opportunities like never before. Among the most exciting domains impacted by this is design. Once a field where expertise was gauged by years of experience and a keen eye for aesthetics, design is now becoming accessible to everyone, thanks to AI.

Gone are the days when you had to either hire a professional designer or spend hours trying to navigate complicated software to produce decent visuals for your business or personal use. With AI-driven design platforms, what used to take hours can now be achieved in minutes. From logo design to web layouts, these platforms are equipped with algorithms trained to produce eye-catching and effective designs based on a few simple prompts.

For example, tools like Canva now offer AI-driven features that help you create custom designs without starting from scratch. Whether it's social media graphics, presentations, or even videos, these platforms can generate various options in a matter of minutes, and all you have to do is choose the one that suits your taste.

AI design platforms are even venturing into more specialized fields like UX/UI design, offering automated solutions that use predictive analytics to determine what design elements work best for your target audience. These platforms can A/B test different designs, learn from user interaction, and continually refine the design to improve performance.

As with any AI technology, the concern for job displacement is legitimate. Does the automation of design services spell the end for professional designers? Not necessarily. While

AI can handle routine tasks and generate basic designs, there's still a need for human creativity to conceive original concepts, especially for more complex projects. In fact, AI can serve as a collaborative tool for designers, taking care of the tedious parts of the job and allowing them to focus on creative and strategic activities.

It's a win-win situation: Businesses save on costs and get quicker results, while designers can elevate their role from mere executors to creative strategists. AI in design services is not a job-killer but a productivity booster. And for individuals or small businesses on a tight budget, it's a game-changer.

By using these automated design services, you're not just saving time and money. You're becoming part of a larger trend that's leveling the playing field, offering high-quality design solutions to everyone, regardless of their skill level or financial capacity.

Healthcare Solutions for Home Use

As we approach a future teeming with technological advancements, the healthcare sector isn't lagging behind. We're living in an age where you no longer have to wait in long queues at a hospital for a check-up or diagnosis. AI is gradually making healthcare accessible right from the comforts of your living room. A host of new startups and established tech companies are launching AI-driven healthcare solutions that can be used at home, making primary care more accessible, quicker, and often, more reliable.

Let's first look at AI-powered diagnostic tools. Imagine a cold winter night where you start to feel sick but dread the thought of going to the ER. Enter AI healthcare apps equipped with symptom checkers. These apps, designed with machine learning algorithms trained on millions of medical cases, can provide instant initial diagnoses based on your symptoms. Whether it's something as trivial as a cold or as serious as a potential cardiac issue, these apps give you an immediate assessment.

But what about ongoing chronic conditions like diabetes or hypertension? Continuous monitoring can be a matter of life and death for people suffering from such diseases. Here, too, AI-based devices are stepping in to fill the gap. Smartwatches and wearable devices equipped with advanced sensors can continuously monitor various health metrics like heart rate, oxygen levels, and even sugar levels for diabetic patients. These wearables can trigger alerts for any abnormal readings, allowing immediate intervention, even predicting potential health crises before they happen.

Furthermore, AI is also helping in treatment recommendations. Apps are being developed that not only diagnose your symptoms but also suggest treatments and even connect you with medical professionals for remote consultations. For instance, you could scan a skin rash using your smartphone, and the app could not only diagnose the condition but also recommend ointments or treatments.

This isn't to say that AI will replace doctors. In contrast, it acts as a bridge to bring specialized medical advice into homes, particularly beneficial for people in remote or underserved areas. It can also free up medical professionals to focus on complex cases, reducing the burden on the healthcare system.

Now, the elephant in the room—data privacy. Medical data is sensitive, and the platforms you use should be HIPAA-compliant or adhere to similar data protection norms. Always check the privacy policies and understand how your data will be used before you start using such services.

AI in healthcare for home use is revolutionary. It is democratizing access to health services, lowering costs, and improving the quality of life. For those with limited mobility, living in remote locations, or even for the busy urban dweller, AI-driven healthcare solutions are making it easier to prioritize health without disrupting daily life.

AI in Agriculture

For the green-thumbed among us, technology might not be the first thing that comes to mind when you're out in your garden or tending to your farm, but AI is set to revolutionize even this most ancient of human activities. Imagine a scenario where your small vegetable patch or large agricultural field could be managed using the predictive algorithms of AI, which could tell you the best time for planting, watering, and even harvesting your crops.

Several companies are leveraging AI to turn agriculture into a high-tech industry, focusing on everything from soil analysis to crop health and automated farming solutions.

These aren't merely lab experiments or theories but real-world applications that are currently in use.

Sensors placed in the soil can measure nutrient levels and moisture content, while drones equipped with AI-powered cameras can scan the field for signs of diseases or pests. The collected data can then be analyzed to offer actionable insights. For example, the AI system might send an alert when the soil is too dry, triggering an automated irrigation system. These technologies can also help farmers decide on the best type of fertilizer to use, based on the nutrient needs of the soil and plants.

AI's predictive analytics can go as far as forecasting the quality of future harvests based on current and historical data. For small-scale gardeners, this could mean knowing when your tomatoes are likely to ripen. For large-scale farmers, this can translate to better yield predictions, which are invaluable for supply chain and price management.

While technology can often seem at odds with something as organic and earthy as farming, the integration of AI into agriculture promises higher yields, reduced waste, and more sustainable farming practices. The environmental benefits are also significant, as better resource management can lead to less waste of water and fertilizers, reducing the ecological footprint of farming operations.

AI is turning agriculture into a data-driven industry, and the early adopters of this technology will undoubtedly reap the benefits. Whether you're a hobbyist gardener or a professional farmer, AI tools can provide invaluable insights that can help improve your yield, make your garden more sustainable, and even predict the quality of your future harvests.

The Gig Economy and AI

We're all familiar with the concept of the gig economy, the modern labor market characterized by short-term contracts or freelance work. While it offers a great deal of flexibility, it's not without its challenges: irregular income, no benefits, and intense competition, to name a few. This is where AI is proving to be a game-changer, enabling gig workers to offer services that were previously the domain of large companies or specialized agencies.

For instance, freelance writers can now utilize AI-based tools for proofreading, SEO optimization, and even content suggestions, enabling them to produce high-quality work more quickly and efficiently. Similar tools exist for freelance graphic designers, programmers, and digital marketers, helping them offer more competitive services and better meet their clients' needs. In some cases, AI can also handle customer service queries, manage schedules, or even help with lead generation, freeing up gig workers to focus on their core services.

This democratization of tools and services through AI is leveling the playing field. It's allowing individual freelancers and small agencies to offer services that were traditionally the realm of larger organizations. For example, data analytics, once a specialized and expensive service, can now be offered by individual freelancers proficient in AI tools designed for this purpose. They can analyze large data sets, produce reports, and even offer predictive analytics services to small and medium-sized businesses that couldn't afford such services from larger organizations.

Furthermore, AI can also aid gig workers in job matching. Several platforms use sophisticated algorithms to match freelancers with suitable jobs based on their skills, experience, and even past client reviews. These algorithms continue to learn from each job match, improving their accuracy over time and increasing the chances that gig workers will get jobs that are an excellent fit for their skill sets.

However, while AI tools offer numerous benefits, they also raise some ethical and practical considerations. For one, the use of AI in the gig economy risks perpetuating a race to the bottom in terms of pricing, as automation makes it easier for freelancers to offer competitive—or even cut-rate—prices. The onus is on the individual to utilize AI responsibly, maintaining a balance between competitive pricing and fair wages.

Moreover, the job-matching algorithms, while generally effective, aren't perfect and may sometimes overlook human factors like work ethic, creativity, or the ability to work well with a team, which can't be easily quantified.

To sum up, AI is profoundly impacting the gig economy, opening up new opportunities but also posing challenges that need to be carefully navigated. The key to success in this new landscape is the intelligent and ethical use of AI tools to enhance one's services and skills, while also keeping in mind the human factors that make each gig worker unique.

Conclusion

As AI continues to evolve, it's penetrating nearly every facet of our lives, making things more efficient, more accessible, and often, more equitable. Whether it's managing your finances, designing a website, diagnosing a medical condition, growing your garden, or finding the perfect gig, AI tools are becoming indispensable. With the correct implementation and ethical considerations, the integration of AI into these various sectors promises not just to make life easier but also to create more opportunities for innovation and inclusivity.

And that brings us to the end of our exploration of how AI is transforming not just industries but also our everyday lives. The takeaway is clear: AI isn't just for companies and scientists; it's for everyone. It's a tool that, when used responsibly and ethically, can significantly amplify our abilities and open up new horizons we've never before thought possible.

The Side Hustle: Earning Extra with AI

You've probably heard the term "side hustle" more times than you can count, but have you ever considered how AI could elevate your side gig to a whole new level? Imagine earning extra income more efficiently, creatively, and smartly. This chapter will delve into the mechanics of transforming a conventional side hustle into an AI-driven enterprise.

Understanding the Side Hustle Landscape in the Age of AI

The very fabric of employment is changing. The days when a single job could provide for all of your needs and wants are slowly fading. A "side hustle" is no longer an option but a necessity for many. But what makes the landscape even more intriguing is the advent of Artificial Intelligence.

The age of AI offers a range of opportunities that could make your side hustle not only more profitable but also more efficient and less time-consuming. With the right kind of AI tool, you could automate mundane tasks, generate insights from data that could help you make better decisions, or even create products or services that are highly customized to individual needs. And the best part? You don't have to be a tech wizard to incorporate AI into your side gig. Numerous platforms and tools are available that make AI technologies accessible to the average person.

One of the most significant advantages of AI is its capacity for data analysis. In the world of investments, for example, AI can churn through years of market data in seconds, spotting trends that would take a human analyst much longer to identify. Several AI-driven investment platforms offer automated trading based on real-time market analysis, substantially reducing the risks while improving the chances of making a profit. Such platforms are democratizing investment opportunities, making what was once accessible only to Wall Street now available to Main Street.

But the applications of AI in side hustles go beyond number-crunching. Creative fields like blogging, photography, and art are also ripe for AI integration. Take blogging, for instance. AI tools can assist you in identifying trending topics, optimizing your blog for search engines, and even suggesting improvements in your writing style. Some AI tools can even auto-generate articles based on the topic and guidelines you provide, although the ethical implications of such a practice are still up for debate.

AI can also be a boon for artists and photographers. There are AI tools designed to enhance photographs, suggest composition improvements, and even help in the actual process of creating art. Artists can use AI algorithms to explore new styles and textures, sometimes resulting in works that are a blend of human creativity and machine-generated complexity.

So how can you differentiate your side hustle in this AI-driven world? The key is to offer something uniquely human, enhanced by the power of AI. Whether you're selling a product or a service, your personal touch—your unique perspective and creativity—will always be your most significant asset. AI can process data, automate tasks, and even create to an extent, but it can't replicate human emotion and creativity. Combining your unique skills with the capabilities of AI can make your side hustle stand out in an increasingly crowded marketplace.

But as with anything, there's a responsible way to incorporate AI into your side hustle. Ethical considerations shouldn't be an afterthought; they should be front and center in your business plan. Whether it's ensuring the data you use is sourced responsibly or being transparent about how you're using AI to enhance your services or products, ethical considerations are paramount. After all, the last thing you want is for your side hustle to become a side hassle.

To sum up, the potential of integrating AI into your side hustle is immense. From automating tasks to generating insights and enhancing creativity, AI has the power to transform your side gig into something much bigger. However, as with any powerful tool, the key to success lies in how you use it. With the right mix of human creativity and machine intelligence, along with a strong ethical framework, your AI-driven side hustle could be your ticket to financial freedom.

Investment Opportunities: From Stocks to Cryptocurrency

In the not-so-distant past, the idea of playing the stock market or dabbling in cryptocurrency seemed like a pursuit reserved for financial gurus or risk-loving speculators. Now, imagine a world where you, with your unique skills but limited finance knowledge, can also join this lucrative game, courtesy of artificial intelligence. If you've ever fantasized about this possibility, your dream could very well become reality.

It starts with a fundamental understanding that AI isn't just a tool; it's an extension of your investment mindset. Think of AI as your 'second brain' for investment—a hyper-efficient one capable of computations and analyses at speeds no human could match. However, instead of replacing your intuition and judgment, AI complements them. It refines your strategy, executes your trades, and most importantly, learns from the patterns it deciphers in stock or cryptocurrency markets.

One exciting development in the field of AI is the "robo-advisor," a tool that uses machine learning to understand the nuances of financial markets. Robo-advisors gather data from multiple sources, such as historical price, market trends, and economic indicators, to name a few. They then process this data in real-time to make predictive analyses and recommendations. What's even more captivating is that many of these robo-advisors adapt to market changes. If a particular investment strategy isn't yielding the expected results, the AI algorithms can shift strategies, all while keeping your financial goals in sight.

But AI's capabilities don't stop at traditional markets like stocks and bonds. They extend into the comparatively wild terrains of cryptocurrencies. A decade ago, the notion of digital currencies was met with skepticism, but today, they've proven to be an asset class of their own. In a market as volatile as cryptocurrency, the quick thinking of an AI can make a significant difference. Algorithms capable of high-frequency trading can execute hundreds of transactions in the time it would take you to blink, exploiting market gaps and making micro-profits that add up over time.

Yet, even with the prodigious capabilities of AI, a level of caution is advised. Though the technology has evolved exponentially, it's not devoid of flaws. Market conditions can change in ways that are impossible to predict—political unrest, natural disasters, or even tweets from influential figures can create unexpected upheavals. AI can analyze patterns and make forecasts based on existing data, but it can't foresee the unforeseeable. Therefore, while you should be willing to trust the efficiency of AI, you should do so with a balanced perspective.

Moreover, consider the fees and the learning curve involved. Not all robo-advisors or AI-driven trading platforms are user-friendly, and some charge hefty fees that could eat into your profits. It's advisable to start small, perhaps with a simulated trading account, to understand the platform's functionalities and the extent of its capabilities and limitations.

So, what does this all mean for someone interested in a side hustle? It means that the playing field is leveling out. With the democratising power of AI, investment is no longer a game for the elite but an opportunity open to all. While the inherent risks of investing still exist, the barriers to entry are significantly lower. You no longer need to spend hours poring over financial statements or keeping up with market news. Your AI assistant can do the heavy lifting, leaving you with more time to focus on strategy, or perhaps, another side hustle.

This shift isn't just an evolution; it's a revolution. And like all revolutions, it promises to change the existing order of things. In this case, it's turning every would-be investor into a potential financial wizard, empowered by the capabilities of artificial intelligence. Whether you're a Wall Street enthusiast or a cryptocurrency maverick, your ability to earn an extra income has been significantly boosted. All you need to do is take that first step into the brave new world of AI-driven investing.

Creative Ventures: AI in Blogging, Photography, and Art

Gone are the days when the word "creative" referred solely to painters, writers, and musicians. Today, creativity has become an interdisciplinary endeavor, and with the integration of AI technologies, the realm of creative pursuits has expanded exponentially. For those with an artistic flair, the melding of creativity and technology is not just a trend but an evolutionary step that promises limitless possibilities.

Let's start with blogging. Writing is one of the oldest forms of expression, but it's also one that's been significantly impacted by the digital age. The concept of blogging exploded in the early 2000s, turning anyone with a computer and an internet connection into a potential writer. But in a world where content is king, quality and consistency are crucial. This is where AI comes into play. Tools like grammar checkers and style editors have long existed, but the new generation of AI writing assistants can do so much more. They can help generate topic ideas, optimize SEO, and even predict how well your blog post will perform based on historical data and current internet trends. Imagine having a tool that analyzes your target audience and recommends not just keywords but also writing styles and even the ideal posting schedule for maximum engagement. The blogosphere is no longer just a space but a dynamic ecosystem, and with AI, you're not just surviving—you're thriving.

If you're into photography, AI offers an equally impressive range of possibilities. Photo editing, a task that used to require hours of manual effort, can now be executed in seconds. From simple tasks like removing red-eye or enhancing color balance to more complex ones like object removal or even style transfer, AI algorithms can perform these operations with startling accuracy. But beyond editing, AI tools can assist you even while capturing the shot. Modern smartphones and professional cameras are integrating AI to recommend the optimal settings based on the surrounding conditions, making sure you get the best shot every time.

In the domain of visual arts like painting or sculpture, AI is doing more than just assisting; it's collaborating. Artists are using AI algorithms to help them conceptualize new pieces, simulate different materials, and even to execute the initial stages of their work. For instance, you can feed your AI tool thousands of art history references, your previous works, and a list of themes or emotions you'd like to explore. The AI then churns out a series of draft concepts for you to refine and finalize. In essence, the AI becomes a part of your creative process, acting as a muse, a critic, and a co-creator, all rolled into one.

This fusion of art and technology is not merely a gimmick; it's a profound transformation of how we conceive and create art. Our creative canvas has expanded, and the tools at our disposal have evolved. Now, artists aren't just limited by their imagination but are empowered by machine intelligence.

As exhilarating as these developments are, they raise essential questions about originality and intellectual property. When you co-create with an AI, who owns the artwork? This is an area still under legal and ethical scrutiny, and if you venture into AI-assisted art, you must tread carefully. Many online platforms offer AI art services, but it's essential to read the fine print about ownership rights before you dive in.

What's undeniable, however, is that AI has and will continue to redefine what it means to be creative. It's a game-changer for professionals and hobbyists alike, leveling the playing field in unprecedented ways. Whether you are a writer, a photographer, or a visual artist, integrating AI into your creative workflow can not only enhance the quality of your work but also expand your artistic horizons. And, as a side hustle, it opens up new avenues for monetization that didn't exist a decade ago.

Small-Scale Business Ventures: Selling AI-Driven Products or Services

The advent of AI is not just transforming large corporations; it's opening new avenues for small-scale entrepreneurs as well. The beautiful thing about today's technology landscape is that AI tools and services have become incredibly accessible. With open-source software, cloud computing, and a wealth of AI APIs, one doesn't need a Ph.D. in computer science to build a business around artificial intelligence.

For instance, consider the realm of customer service, a field traditionally reliant on human intervention. With chatbots and automated service platforms powered by AI, a small business can offer 24/7 customer support without maintaining a large staff. A flower shop could employ a chatbot to handle customer inquiries about flower availability, prices, and delivery options. This chatbot could learn from previous customer interactions to provide increasingly sophisticated and accurate responses, saving time and improving the user experience. With the right marketing and quality of service, this flower shop could distinguish itself in a crowded market simply by utilizing AI.

Or take the case of marketing analysis. Small businesses often can't afford to hire teams of analysts to sift through consumer data. However, they can subscribe to AI services that can perform the same functions at a fraction of the cost. These platforms can generate customer profiles, recommend targeted marketing campaigns, and even predict future buying trends, empowering a small-scale entrepreneur to make data-driven decisions.

Retail is another sector where AI can have a transformative impact. Imagine a small bookstore using AI to manage its inventory. By analyzing sales data, online reviews, and even local cultural events (like author talks or book fairs), the AI system can recommend which books to stock up on and which to phase out. The bookstore owner can thus minimize unsold inventory, improve turnover, and maximize profits.

Beyond the traditional business sectors, AI also enables completely new types of products and services. Think about personalized content curation as a service, where an AI engine sorts through the vast ocean of online articles, videos, podcasts, and more, to deliver a personalized reading list or entertainment queue for individual customers. The same engine could also recommend learning paths for students, vacation itineraries for travelers, or even workout and meal plans for health-conscious individuals. The possibilities are boundless.

When considering a small-scale business venture powered by AI, the first step is to identify a problem that AI can solve efficiently. Next, explore the available technologies that can be used to solve this problem. This could involve some learning, or perhaps even a partnership with someone who has the necessary technical skills. Once you have a working prototype, test it rigorously, refine it based on feedback, and then plan your market entry strategy.

The costs of setting up an AI-based service have plummeted in recent years. Platforms like AWS and Google Cloud offer scalable solutions where you only pay for the computational resources you use. Open-source libraries for machine learning and natural language processing can give you a head start in developing your system. However, as with any business, an AI-driven venture requires careful planning, a clear understanding of the market, and a relentless focus on customer experience.

And, as always, consider the ethical ramifications of your business. If your AI platform will handle user data, how will you ensure privacy and security? What are the potential biases in your AI model, and how will you mitigate them? Ethical business practices are not just a moral imperative but also a competitive advantage in today's discerning market.

Small-scale doesn't mean small impact. In a world increasingly driven by AI, even the tiniest enterprise can leverage this technology to offer something extraordinary. With smart planning and ethical practices, your small-scale AI business venture could become the next big thing.

How to Differentiate Your Side Hustle with AI

The gig economy has grown exponentially over the past decade. It offers an attractive proposition: freedom, flexibility, and the ability to earn income on your own terms. The flip side, however, is the intense competition that freelancers and gig workers face. With millions of people offering similar services, standing out is not just an advantage; it's a necessity. One of the ways to gain that competitive edge is by leveraging Artificial Intelligence in your side hustle.

Imagine you're a freelance graphic designer. While your human creativity is irreplaceable, there are routine tasks that take up a lot of your time—like image resizing, color adjustments, or even initial mockups. By automating these mundane tasks through AI tools, you not only free up your time but also reduce the margin for human error. This allows you to focus more on creative tasks and take up more projects, thereby increasing your earning potential. Your USP becomes 'designs backed by data-driven AI analysis for optimal user engagement,' rather than just 'aesthetically pleasing designs.'

Similarly, suppose you're into freelance content creation or copywriting. AI tools like grammar checkers or style analyzers can make your writing crisp and error-free. More advanced AI models can analyze the SEO effectiveness of your content, suggest improvements, or even recommend topics that are currently trending in your domain. When pitching to clients, you're not just selling your writing services; you're offering a comprehensive, AI-backed content strategy.

For those in consulting or coaching, AI can offer an unprecedented level of personalized service. You could use machine learning algorithms to analyze the performance metrics of a business over multiple parameters, offering insights and solutions tailored specifically for that business. On the personal coaching side, AI can track the progress of your clients and suggest changes in real-time, significantly increasing the effectiveness of your program.

Even in physical jobs like carpentry or house painting, AI can help you stand out. For instance, image recognition software can instantly provide measurements and suggest the optimal use of space or materials. AI tools can analyze previous work samples and customer reviews to identify styles or techniques that have been particularly well-received, guiding your future projects.

But how do you get started? First, identify the area within your side hustle that can be enhanced or made more efficient through AI. You don't need to become an AI expert overnight. There are many tools, both free and subscription-based, designed for people without a tech background. Start by incorporating one or two of these into your workflow and measuring the impact. Use the results as a selling point when you market your services.

The next phase is to think big. Once you're comfortable with basic AI tools, consider more advanced applications. This might require teaming up with an AI developer or taking a few online courses to deepen your understanding. Remember, the goal is to provide a service that few others can, and advanced AI applications can help you do exactly that.

Differentiating your side hustle is not just about incorporating AI but doing it in a way that aligns with what you're good at and what your clients need. It involves constant learning, adaptation, and sometimes even challenging the norms of your domain. So go ahead, let AI be the rocket fuel for your side hustle, and watch your small venture take giant strides.

Safety and Ethics: Responsible Use of AI in Your Side Hustle

As we journey through the potential that AI holds for amplifying your side hustle, there's a responsibility that comes with this powerful technology. It's not just about how AI can help you generate income; it's also about how you wield this tool in a way that is ethical, safe, and respectful of both laws and individual privacy.

In the exhilarating rush to capitalize on AI's capabilities, it's easy to overlook its ethical implications. For instance, using AI to scrape personal information from social media profiles for targeted marketing may give you a business advantage, but it also poses serious ethical and legal questions. Likewise, if your AI tool is analyzing consumer behavior, how much of that data do you own? What are you allowed to do with it? These questions are not merely theoretical; they have real-world consequences that can affect your business and reputation.

In healthcare or wellness coaching, using AI algorithms to diagnose or recommend treatments can be a slippery slope. Any inaccuracies can not only get you into legal trouble but could also potentially risk lives. Thus, it's imperative that you consult with professionals in the respective field to ensure that your AI tools meet the necessary standards for accuracy and reliability.

Similarly, if your side hustle involves creating or selling AI-powered surveillance equipment, it's essential to understand the legal implications. For instance, facial recognition software can be a potent tool in security, but it also raises significant privacy concerns. Ensure your products comply with laws concerning data collection and privacy.

But safety and ethics go beyond just compliance with laws. Ethical AI usage in your side hustle is also about how your services impact society at large. For example, if your AI-driven content creation tool is capable of producing articles, what happens when it writes something that is factually incorrect or promotes misinformation? Your responsibility extends to correcting such errors and ensuring that your AI tools are trained to be as accurate as possible.

Moreover, the AI you employ should be designed and trained to be unbiased. Whether you're using AI for HR recruiting services, loan approvals in your fintech startup, or customer service, the algorithms should not discriminate based on race, gender, or any other factor. Ensuring your AI tool is unbiased requires regular auditing and perhaps consultation with experts in the field of AI ethics.

Finally, let's talk about transparency. Your clients have a right to know when and how you're using AI in your services. Whether it's ·through clear disclaimers, detailed terms of service, or direct communication, transparency builds trust. It assures your clients that while you're using advanced technology to enhance your services, you're doing so in a manner that respects their rights and safety.

As we close the chapter on using AI for your side hustle, it's clear that the landscape of opportunities is as vast as it is complex. But as you've seen throughout this book, the rewards—both financial and personal—can be tremendous when you approach AI with a discerning and responsible mindset. While we've touched upon a multitude of topics, from the birth and growth of AI startups to the individual opportunities for skills enhancement and side hustles, the journey doesn't end here. In the concluding chapter, we'll tie together the key takeaways and offer a roadmap for your ongoing journey in the world of AI. It's a world that is ever-evolving, and the only constant is the need for continuous learning and adaptation. So, let's look back and forge ahead, as we wrap up our comprehensive exploration of how AI can transform your world.

Conclusion

From the embryonic stage of understanding the foundations of AI, to the sprawling applications in startups and businesses, and eventually down to the individual scale where AI can function as a virtual co-worker—this book has been a comprehensive odyssey into the transformative world of Artificial Intelligence. You've been led through the intricacies of AI's capabilities, its ethical implications, and the vast horizon of opportunities it has unveiled in various sectors like healthcare, finance, agriculture, and even in augmenting personal skills.

You discovered how AI is not just an abstract tech concept but a tangible tool, capable of revolutionizing industries. The book dissected various facets of machine learning, data science, and AI ethics, grounding the high-flying concepts in concrete examples and case studies. We looked at how entrepreneurs have struck gold by harnessing AI's capabilities, creating ventures that not only generated capital but also added immeasurable value to society. The book served as a canvas, painting a vivid portrait of AI's role in making businesses more efficient, ventures more lucrative, and personal lives more enriched.

We unraveled the journey of startups, from inception to scaling, offering you a playbook filled with actionable insights. You saw how practical, ground-level considerations in sectors as varied as agriculture and healthcare are on the cusp of a technological revolution. We demystified complex concepts, breaking them down into bite-sized, easily digestible pieces that anyone—whether a tech novice or a seasoned pro—can understand. This book wasn't just about what AI can do; it's also a narrative about what you can do with AI.

The reality of AI is that it's a tool—a highly sophisticated one, yes, but in the end, its utility is determined by the hands that wield it. Just like a canvas remains a piece of fabric until a painter transforms it into art, AI's potential remains untapped until you apply it. There will be struggles, just as any painter faces the daunting blank canvas or any entrepreneur confronts the fear of the unknown. But the rewards, both tangible and intangible, make the challenges worth it. The journey through the landscapes of AI is as thrilling as the destinations it can take you to. So why just read about it when you can live it?

Your next step in the incredible journey of AI starts now. Whether it's launching your startup, scaling your business, or even automating your gardening, the next step is yours to take. Envision a world where your skills are amplified by AI, where your business operates at peak efficiency, and where your contributions have a ripple effect of positive change.

That world is not a fantasy; it's a future that's yours to shape. Don't just let this book be a source of knowledge; let it be a call to action. The best time to act is now.

For those who wish to delve deeper, here are some resources that can further aid your journey into the world of AI:

1. "Artificial Intelligence: A Guide to Intelligent Systems" - Book for foundational knowledge. [URL]

2. Coursera's AI For Everyone - An online course designed for non-technical people. [URL]

3. TED Talks on AI - For various perspectives and ethical considerations. [URL]

4. GitHub Repositories - For AI enthusiasts who want to get their hands dirty with code. [URL]

5. AI Ethics Guidelines by [Institution] - To keep you grounded in responsible AI usage. [URL]

You're not just a reader but a participant in the AI revolution. The canvas is broad; the palette is rich. It's time to create your masterpiece.

About the Author

Brendan has been in the tech game for over 20 years, and he's seen it all. From the early days of clunky desktop computers to today's world of smart homes and smarter phones, he's been right there, rolling up his sleeves and figuring out how to make technology work better for everyone. He's led teams at big-name tech companies and launched startups from his garage. In other words, he's got the experience to back up what he says.

But what really sets Brendan apart is his belief that AI is for everyone. He knows that this technology has the power to change lives, and he's committed to making sure it does. That's why he's not just writing for tech experts. His book is a practical guide aimed at everyone—from business owners to regular folks who just want to make their lives a bit easier.

When he's not writing or diving into the latest AI research, Brendan is all about giving back. He sits on the boards of nonprofits that are getting young people excited about science and tech, and he's a regular at schools and community events, talking about the positive impact of AI.

Enjoyed the Book? I'd Love to Hear from You!

I want to thank you for taking the time to read my book. I truly hope it has empowered you to embrace the transformative power of AI in your life and business. Your feedback means the world to me and it helps others discover this resource too.

Your honest review helps the book reach more people and make a bigger impact. If you've found the book helpful, insightful, or inspiring, I'd be super grateful if you could take a couple of minutes to leave a review on Amazon.

Just scan the QR code above with your phone's camera to jump directly to the review page.

Your words could be the encouragement someone else needs to pick up the book and make meaningful changes in their life. Thank you for your time and your support!